THE 100+ SERIES™

Reproducible Activities

Using the Standards

Problem Solving

Grade 5

By

P. A. M. Howard

Published by Instructional Fair
an imprint of
Frank Schaffer Publications®

W9-CQY-367

Instructional Fair

Author: P. A. M. Howard
Editors: Melissa Warner Hale and Linda Triemstra

Frank Schaffer Publications®

Instructional Fair is an imprint of Frank Schaffer Publications.

Send all inquiries to:
Frank Schaffer Publications
3195 Wilson Drive NW
Grand Rapids, Michigan 49534

Using the Standards—Problem Solving—grade 5

ISBN: 0-7424-1825-1

5 6 7 8 9 10 PAT 09 08 07

Table of Contents

Introduction 4–5

NCTM Standards
Correlation Chart 6

Problem-Solving
Challenge 7–8

Number and Operations
A Slice of the Pie 9
Freaky Fractions 10
Even or Odd? 11
Finding Factors 12
Positively Prime 13
Which Is More? 14
Distance, Rate, and Time . . . 15
Multiplication
   Madness 16–17
Supermarket Dilemma 18
Candy Bar Calculations 19
Pleasantville Elementary 20
Pleading the Fifth 21
How Many? 22–23
Parking Problems 24
Pizza! Pizza! Pizza! 25
Nature Camp 26–27
Toys, Toys, Toys 28
Is It Enough? 29
Planning a Picnic 30–31
Create Your
   Own Problems 32
Check Your Skills 33

Algebra
Shape Patterns 34
Function Machine 35
Do the Two-Step 36
Number Patterns 37
More Number Patterns 38
Who's Taller? 39

All About Order 40
Missing Numbers 41–43
Finding Unknowns 44
Making Equations 45–46
Tall Towers 47–48
Show Me the Money! . . 49–50
Growing Patterns 51
Create Your
   Own Problems 52
Check Your Skills 53

Geometry
A Class by Itself 54–55
Pondering Polygons 56
Parallelograms 57
Quadrilaterals 58
Angle Sums 59–60
Prisms and Pyramids 61
Plotting Pleasantville 62–63
Finding Routes 64–65
Line Symmetry 66
Reflections 67
Rotations 68
Translations 69
Toothpick Troubles 70
Mosaic Madness 71
Tiling Patterns 72
To Tile or Not to Tile . . . 73–74
Timely Tiling 75
Create Your
   Own Problems 76
Check Your Skills 77

Measurement
Estimating Will Do 78–79
Fencing In 80
Rectangular Reasoning . 81–82
Confounding Confetti 83
Calling All Units 84

A Matter of Time 85
The Temperature Is Rising . . 86
Weighty Matters 87
Lively Liquids 88
The Better Buy 89
Create Your
   Own Problems 90
Check Your Skills 91

Data Analysis and Probability
At the Movies 92
Favorite Sport 93
How Do You Get
   to School? 94
Favorite Season 95
Everyone's a Critic 96
In the News 97
Test Scores 98
Standing in Line 99–100
Keep on Rolling 101
Random Draw 102
Spin Out 103
Create Your
   Own Problems 104
Check Your Skills 105

Cumulative
Post-Test 106–107

Pattern Block
Templates 108–109

Dollar Bill Templates 110

Answer Key 111–120

Vocabulary Cards . . 121–128

Published by Instructional Fair. Copyright Protected.

0-7424-1825-1 *Problem Solving*

Introduction

This book is designed around NCTM standards with a focus on [puzzle icon] problem solving. Students will build new mathematical knowledge, solve problems in context, apply and adapt appropriate strategies, and reflect on the problem-solving process. At the same time, students will utilize skills from the NCTM content standards: Number and Operations, Algebra, Geometry, Measurement, and Data Analysis and Probability. The other NCTM process standards—Reasoning and Proof [magnifying glass icon], Communication [pencil icon], Connections [phone icon], and Representation [triangle icon]—are also incorporated throughout the activities. The correlation chart on page 6 identifies the pages on which each NCTM standard appears.

Problem-Solving Challenge: This short pretest contains a representative sampling of problem-solving activities similar to those used throughout this book. Give this pretest at one time, or present one problem at a time over a series of days. Teachers may choose to assign these problems to individuals, pairs, or groups.

The purpose of the pretest is to provide insights into the thought processes and strategies students already possess. The emphasis should not be on the number of "right" answers. Instead, encourage students to try their best and write down their ideas. These problems can also provide opportunities for class discussion as students share their thought processes with one another.

Workbook Pages: These activities can be done independently, in pairs, or in groups. Guided activities lead students through problem-solving strategies. Then, students have the opportunity to choose one of these strategies to solve similar types of problems. Since the emphasis is on problem solving rather than computation, calculators may be used to complete some exercises.

Problems may be broken into parts, with class discussion following student work. Students may be more successful if they understand the guided problem before attempting the independent problems. Students may gravitate toward using the strategy presented in the guided problems, but they should also be encouraged to create their own strategies.

Many activities will lead into subjects that could be investigated or discussed further as a class. Compare different solution methods or discuss how to select a valid solution method for a particular problem.

0-7424-1825-1 *Problem Solving*

Introduction (cont.)

Communication: Each activity ends with a communication section. These questions may be used as journal prompts, writing activities, or discussion prompts. Each communicatin question is labeled: reflecting, organizing, expanding, comparing, describing, or explaining.

Check Your Skills: These activities provide a representative sample of the types of processes and skills developed throughout each content section. This can be used as additional practice or as a post-test.

Cumulative Post-Test: This short post test provides a representative sample of content from all sections of the book. It may be used for assessment or extra practice. The test can be given all at one time or may be split up over several days.

Vocabulary Cards: Use the vocabulary cards to familiarize students with mathematical language. The pages may be copied, cut, and pasted onto index cards. Paste the front and back on the same index card to make flash cards, or paste each side on separate cards to use in matching games and activities.

Assessment: Assessment is an integral part of the learning process and can include observations, conversations, interviews, interactive journals, writing prompts, and independent quizzes or tests. Classroom discussions help students learn the difference between poor, good, and excellent responses. Scoring guides can help analyze students' responses. The following is one possible scoring rubric. Modify this rubric as necessary to fit specific problems.

1—student understands the problem and knows what he/she is being asked to find

2—student selects an appropriate strategy or process to solve the problem

3—student is able to model the problem with appropriate graphs, tables, pictures, computations, or equations

4—student is able to clearly explain or demonstrate his/her thinking and reasoning

Published by Instructional Fair. Copyright Protected.

0-7424-1825-1 *Problem Solving*

NCTM Standards Correlation Chart

		Problem Solving	Reasoning and Proof	Connections	Representation
Number & Operations	number systems		11, 12, 13	9, 41	10
	operations	14		15, 16, 17, 18, 24, 25, 41, 42, 43, 94, 95	16, 17
	computations & estimation		26	19, 22, 23, 26, 27, 28, 29, 30, 31	20, 21
Algebra	patterns, relations, & functions	35, 36, 37, 38	39, 40	34, 47, 48	
	situations & structures; symbols	44		16, 17, 41, 42, 43	44, 44, 42, 43
	mathematical models			45, 47, 48, 60	45, 46, 47, 48
	change in context	51		49, 50	49, 50
Geometry	properties of two- & three-dimensional shapes	56, 57, 58, 61	54, 55, 59, 60	45, 47, 48, 60	
	coordinate geometry	62, 63, 69		64, 65	64
	transformations & symmetry	66, 67, 68, 69			
	visualization, spatial reasoning, & geometric modeling	70, 75	72, 73, 74	34, 71	
Measurement	units, systems, & processes of measurement	78, 79	84	80, 83	
	techniques, tools, & formulas	85, 87, 88	81, 82	80, 81, 82, 83, 86, 89, 94, 95	
Data Analysis & Probability	collect, organize, & display data			93, 94, 95	92, 93
	statistical methods to analyze data	97, 98		93, 95	92, 93, 96
	data inferences and predictions				
	basic concepts of probability	99, 100, 101, 102, 103			

*All pages are problem solving. Pages listed as problem solving in the chart are those that do not also contain one of the other three process strands.

**The Problem Solving Challenge, Create Your Own Problems, Check Your Skills, and Cumulative Post-Test pages are not included on this chart but contain a representative sampling of all content and process standards.

The NCTM communication process strand is found at the end of each activity.

Problem-Solving Challenge

Answer the following questions on a separate sheet of paper.

1. The decimal value of $\frac{1}{6}$ is about 0.167. Estimate the decimal values of $\frac{2}{6}$, $\frac{4}{6}$, and $\frac{5}{6}$. Then write the equivalent percentage for each. Show your work.

2. Which is more, 20 boxes of 13 candy bars or 15 boxes of 18 candy bars? How do you know?

3. What is another way to calculate 8 x 5, using only multiplication? Draw a model that shows both expressions are the same.

4. The Super Savings Department Store is having a sale. Everything is 40% off the regular price. Luiza wants to buy a pair of jeans, regularly priced at $65. Sales tax is 6%. How much will the jeans cost?

5. Discount Wheels has 2,500 hubcaps in stock. How many cars and trucks could get new hubcaps before the store runs out? Show your work.

6. Fill in the table. Write the rule.

IN	2	3	6	9	11
OUT	16	24	48		

Rule: _____

7. Find the value of each shape.

    a. $6 \times \blacktriangle = 72$

    b. $\bullet \div 7 = 126$

    c. $55 - 6 = 7 \times \blacksquare$

0-7424-1825-1 *Problem Solving*

Problem-Solving Challenge (cont.)

8. A box has a square base with a side length of 5 inches. Let **H** be the height of the box, in inches. Write an equation that shows how to find the number of 1-inch cubes, **C**, that would fit in the box. Explain why your equation works. What type of measurement is **C**?

9. What are the defining characteristics of a parallelogram?

10. How can you use angle measurements to decide whether or not a group of shapes will create a tiling pattern?

11. How many 3" by 5" index cards will fit on a 5' by 2' surface? Show your work.

12. About how many centimeters are in 5 inches? Show your work.

13. Mr. Jackson's car uses 36 gallons of gas a week. How many liters of gas is this?

14. A whale weighs 6,500 kg. How many tons is this? Show your work.

15. Here are 19 test scores. Find the median and the first and third quartiles. Explain what these numbers tell you about how students did on the test.

73, 45, 91, 75, 61, 80, 80, 52, 66, 95, 85, 63, 90, 65, 90, 74, 94, 77, 81

16. There are 12 cubes in a bag. A green cube is most likely to be drawn. There is an equal chance of drawing a blue or orange cube. A yellow cube is least likely to be drawn. There is a better chance of drawing a red cube than a blue cube. How many cubes of each color are in the bag?

 0-7424-1825-1 *Problem Solving*

Name _____ Date _____

A Slice of the Pie

1. Write the fraction and its decimal equivalent for each shaded section of the circle.

_____ _____ _____

_____ _____ _____

_____ _____ _____

2. Mark the location of each fraction on the number line.

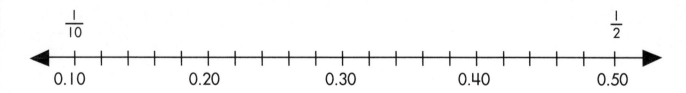

$\frac{1}{10}$ .... $\frac{1}{2}$

0.10   0.20   0.30   0.40   0.50

REFLECTING

As the denominator of the fraction gets larger, what happens to the value of the fraction? Describe the pattern. Why does this happen?

0-7424-1825-1 *Problem Solving*

Name _____ Date _____

Freaky Fractions

$$\frac{1}{2} = 0.5 \qquad \frac{1}{3} \approx 0.33 \qquad \frac{1}{4} = 0.25 \qquad \frac{1}{5} = 0.20 \qquad \frac{1}{6} \approx 0.17$$

1. Estimate the decimal equivalent of $\frac{2}{3}$ without using long division or a calculator. Show your work.

2. Estimate the decimal equivalent of $\frac{2}{5}$, $\frac{3}{5}$, and $\frac{4}{5}$ without using long division or a calculator. Show your work.

3. Estimate the decimal equivalent of $\frac{2}{6}$, $\frac{3}{6}$, $\frac{4}{6}$, and $\frac{5}{6}$ without using long division or a calculator. Show your work.

4. Insert the correct sign (**< > =**) between each pair of fractions.

    a. $\frac{2}{3}$ $\frac{3}{5}$ **b.** $\frac{2}{5}$ $\frac{1}{3}$

    c. $\frac{3}{4}$ $\frac{4}{5}$ **d.** $\frac{3}{5}$ $\frac{1}{2}$

EXPLAINING

Explain the method you used to solve problem 4. Compare solution methods with your classmates.

0-7424-1825-1 *Problem Solving*

Name _____ Date _____

Even or Odd?

1. Make a **hypothesis**. The product of 2 even numbers is _____ .

2. **Test** your hypothesis. Multiply several pairs of even numbers. Be sure to use a variety of large and small numbers.

3. **Prove** or **disprove** your hypothesis. Include evidence. Explain your reasoning.

4. Make and test hypotheses about the product of 2 odd numbers and the product of an even and an odd number. Find a hypothesis you can prove to be true.

REFLECTING

How much evidence is needed to disprove a hypothesis?
How much evidence is needed to prove a hypothesis?

0-7424-1825-1 *Problem Solving*

Name _____ Date _____

Finding Factors

Materials: 100 chart

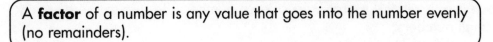

A **factor** of a number is any value that goes into the number evenly (no remainders).

There are several "tricks" for finding factors of large numbers. You may be familiar with some of them already.

1. Complete the following statements.

   a. A number will have a factor of 2 if _____ .

   b. A number will have a factor of 5 if _____ .

   c. A number will have a factor of 10 if _____ .

2. Circle all the multiples of 3 on the 100 chart. Find the sum of the digits in each multiple of 3. What do you notice?

3. Put a square around all the multiples of 9 on the 100 chart. Find the sum of the digits in each multiple of 9. What do you notice?

4. Trick: *A number will have a factor of 4 if 4 is a factor of the last 2 digits of the number.* Which of the following numbers have a factor of 4? Use the "trick." Then test the trick. Divide each of the numbers by 4. Does the "trick" work for each number?

   128   2,464   272   346   388   2,300   718   4,512

EXPANDING

Use the 100 chart to examine multiples of 6, 7, and 8. Can you find any patterns? Do you think there is a "trick" for each number?

12

Name _____ Date _____

Positively Prime

> A **prime** number's only factors are one and itself.

1. Can an even number be prime? Explain.

2. Are all odd numbers prime? Explain.

3. Is the product of 2 prime numbers also prime? Explain.

4. Look at a multiplication table. What can you say about the numbers inside the table?

5. Consider the number 143.

    a. Is 2 a factor? _____

    b. Is 3, 6, or 9 a factor? _____

    c. Is 4 or 8 a factor? _____

    d. Is 5 or 10 a factor? _____

    e. Is 7 a factor? _____

    f. Do you think 143 is prime? _____

    g. Try dividing 143 by prime numbers larger than 10. Can you find a factor?

    h. Is 143 prime? _____

6. Find all the prime numbers between 2 and 100. How do you know the numbers are prime?

EXPLAINING

Explain your strategy for deciding whether or not a number is prime.
Do you use any "tricks" to save time?

0-7424-1825-1 *Problem Solving*

Name _____ Date _____

Which Is More?

1. Which is more—

    a. 15 boxes of 18 suckers or 12 boxes of 24 chocolate bars?

    b. How do you know?

2. Which is more—

    a. 12 bags of 30 buttons or 16 bags of 25 buttons?

    b. How do you know?

3. Which is larger—

    a. the rectangular room that is 12 ft. by 14 ft.
    or the one that is 15 ft. by 11 ft.?

    b. How do you know?

REFLECTING

What operation did you use to find the answers?

0-7424-1825-1 *Problem Solving*

Distance, Rate, and Time

Distance = Rate x Time

1. Brianna rode her bike at an average **rate** of 10.8 mph. It took her 2.5 hours to ride to her grandmother's house.

a. How far away does her grandmother live? Show your work.

b. What math operation did you use to find the answer?

2. On the return trip, Brianna averaged only 9 mph. To find the **time** of her trip, the problem needs to be worked backwards.

a. How long did it take Brianna to get home? Show your work.

b. Does your answer make sense?

c. Write an equation showing how to find the **time** if the **distance** and **rate** are known.

Time = _____

REFLECTING

How are the two equations related?

0-7424-1825-1 *Problem Solving*

Name _____ Date _____

Multiplication Madness

1. Write the number sentence that models each picture.

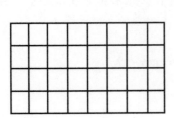

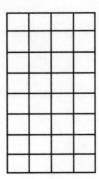

a. 8 x 4 = _____   **b.** _____

2. Julia collects seashells. She has 5 boxes, each holding 3 shells.

a. How many shells does Julia have? _____

b. Write a number sentence that models the problem.

_____

c. Draw a picture to show how she could arrange the shells if she had only 3 boxes.

d. Write a number sentence that models the problem.

_____

REFLECTING

How are the number sentences in problem 1 related?
How are the number sentences in problems 2b and 2d related?

16

Multiplication Madness

1. Write the number sentences that model the picture.

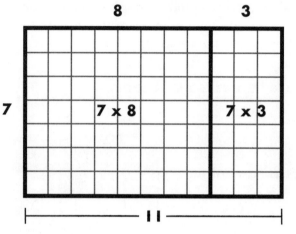

a. 7 x 11 = _____

b. 7 x ___ + 7 x ____ = ____

c. What do you notice about the answers to both number sentences?

2. On a separate piece of graph paper, draw a picture that shows 5 x 13 = _____.

a. Show how you can divide the rectangle into 2 smaller rectangles. Write the number sentence that models the picture.

b. Divide the rectangle differently and write the number sentence.

c. What is true about the answers to each number sentence?

EXPANDING

What's another way to calculate 6 x 14, using multiplication and addition?

0-7424-1825-1 *Problem Solving*

Name _____ Date _____

Supermarket Dilemma

A number of people complained to a supermarket manager that milk purchased from his store was spoiling before the expiration date. The manager called each customer to explain the refrigeration problem and to offer each a free carton of milk. He spent an equal number of minutes on the phone with each customer. He spoke on the phone for a combined total of 3 hours.

1. What is the greatest number of people he could have talked to? Explain.

2. What is the smallest number of people he could have talked to? Explain.

3. How many people did he call if he spent 20 minutes talking to each person? Show your work.

4. How many people did he call if he spent 3 minutes talking to each person? Show your work.

5. How long was each phone conversation if he talked to 45 customers? Show your work.

EXPANDING

Make up your own problem dealing with the time it takes to complete a number of tasks.

0-7424-1825-1 *Problem Solving*

Name _____ Date _____

Candy Bar Calculations

There are 54 candy bars in each box. There are 48 boxes in each
carton. There are 105 cartons in each warehouse.

1. Use rounding to estimate the number of candy bars in one warehouse.
Show your work.

2. One store orders 1,000 candy bars. How many boxes will be needed to ship the bars?
Will all of the boxes be full? Explain.

3. Another store orders 3,000 candy bars. How many cartons and boxes will be needed
for the shipment? Explain.

4. How many candy bars will be stored in 10 warehouses? Show your work.

EXPLAINING

What kinds of questions can be answered using
multiplication? Division?

0-7424-1825-1 *Problem Solving*

Name _____ Date _____

Pleasantville Elementary

The model below shows the number of students in Enrico's class.

1. $\frac{5}{6}$ of the students have brown hair.

   a. The 6 tells you how many **equal sets** were made. Circle 6 equal sets.

   b. How many students were in each set? What fraction of the students is this?

   c. The 5 tells you how many sets have brown hair. How many students is this? Explain.

2. On separate piece of paper, draw another model to show the number of students in the class.

   a. $\frac{2}{5}$ of the class are girls. Are there more girls or more boys in the class? How do you know?

   b. How many equal sets need to be made? Circle the equal sets and tell how many students are in each set.

   c. How many sets are girls? How many girls are in the class? Explain.

REFLECTING

How does drawing a picture help you solve the problem?

20

Name _____ Date _____

Pleading the Fifth

> A **percent** tells how many out of 100 equal parts.
>
> $$20\% = \frac{20}{100} = \frac{2}{10}$$

1. Look at the bar.

   a. What fraction of the bar is shaded? _____

   b. Draw lines to divide the bar into tenths. Write the fraction in tenths. _____

   c. How many hundredths would this be? _____

   d. What percentage of the bar is shaded? _____

2. What percentage is equal to $\frac{2}{5}$?

$\frac{2}{5} = \frac{1}{5} +$ _____ $=$ _____% $+$ _____% $=$ _____%

3. What percentage is equal to $\frac{3}{5}$? $\frac{4}{5}$? Show your work.

EXPANDING

The fraction $\frac{1}{3}$ is approximately 33%.
What percentage would be equal to $\frac{2}{3}$? Explain.

0-7424-1825-1 *Problem Solving*

Name _____ Date _____

How Many?

> To find the **percentage** of an amount, multiply the decimal equivalent by the amount.
>
> To find the **fraction** of an amount, multiply the fraction by the amount.

There are 80 students at Pleasantville Elementary going on field trips.

1. One-quarter of the students are going to the science museum.

    a. How many students is this?

        $\frac{1}{4} \times 80 =$ _____

    b. What percentage is this? _____

2. Forty percent of the students are going to the art museum.

    a. How many students is this?

        $0.40 \times 80 =$ _____

    b. What fraction is this? _____

3. The remaining students are going to the zoo.

    a. What percentage is this? _____

    b. What fraction is this? _____

    c. How many students is this? _____

EXPLAINING

How did you find your answers to problem 3?

22

Name _____ Date _____

How Many?

To find the **percentage** of an amount, multiply the decimal equivalent by the amount.

To find the **fraction** of an amount, multiply the fraction by the amount

There are 300 students attending Pleasantville Elementary School.

1. One-third of the students take the bus to school. How many students is this? Show your work.

2. One-quarter of the students ride in a car to school. How many students is this? Show your work.

3. Two-fifths of the students walk to school. How many students is this? Show your work.

4. The remaining students ride their bikes to school.

   a. How many students is this? Show your work.

   b. What fraction of the students is this? How do you know?

EXPANDING

Find the percentage of students who walk, ride a bus, ride a bike, and ride in a car. What do you get when you add these percentages together? Why does that make sense?

0-7424-1825-1 *Problem Solving*

Name _____ Date _____

Parking Problems

There are a total of 2,400 tires on vehicles in a parking lot.

1. What is the maximum number of cars that could be parked there? Show your work.

2. If $\frac{1}{12}$ of the tires belong to motorcycles, how many motorcycles are in the parking lot? Show your work.

3. There are four 18-wheeler tractor trailers in the parking lot. How many tires belong to tractor trailers? Show your work.

4. The remainder of the tires belong to cars, trucks, minivans, or SUVs. How many of these vehicles are in the parking lot? Show your work.

EXPLAINING

Explain how to combine your answers from problems 2 through 4 to check your work.

0-7424-1825-1 *Problem Solving*

Pizza! Pizza! Pizza!

There are 3 pizzas of different sizes. One has been cut into 12 pieces, one into 9 pieces, and the third into 15 pieces. All the slices are the same size.

1. How would you split the pizza evenly among 9 people? Would there be any pizza left over? Explain.

2. How would you split the pizza evenly among 10 people? Would there be any pizza left over? Explain.

3. Debra ate 4 pieces. What fraction of the slices did she eat?

4. Rayshawn ate $\frac{1}{3}$ of the slices. How many pieces did he eat? Show your work.

5. What fraction of the pizza is left after Debra and Rayshawn ate their pieces? How many pieces are left?

6. There are 4 more people who will eat pizza. Will they be able to split the remaining pieces evenly? Explain.

REFLECTING

Which of these problems was easiest for you to solve? Which was most difficult?

0-7424-1825-1 *Problem Solving*

Name _____ Date _____

Nature Camp

Two fifth-grade classes from Pleasantville Elementary are going to an overnight nature camp. They will spend 2 nights and 3 days at the camp.

1. The trip will cost $75 per student. A total of $4,200 is collected. How many students will be going on the trip? Show your work.

2. All the boys will be sleeping in Cougar Cabin. The girls will be sleeping in Bear Bungalow.

   a. $\frac{4}{7}$ of the students are boys. There are 20 bunks in Cougar Cabin. Will there be enough beds for each boy? Explain.

   b. How many bunks will be needed in Bear Bungalow? Explain.

   c. Draw a picture to prove that your answers are correct.

DESCRIBING

Describe how to find a fraction of an amount.

0-7424-1825-1 *Problem Solving*

Name _____ Date _____

Nature Camp

Two fifth-grade classes from Pleasantville Elementary are going to an overnight nature camp. They will spend 3 days and 2 nights at the camp. There are a total of 80 people going to the camp.

1. Staff, teachers, and parent volunteers make up 15% of the people going to the camp.

    a. How many of the people at the camp are adults? Explain.

    b. How many are campers? Explain.

2. The volunteers will be preparing the meals and snacks. Three meals a day are needed for everyone.

    a. How many meals will need to be prepared? Show your work.

    b. For breakfast, 2 eggs per person are used. How many dozen eggs will be needed? Show your work.

REFLECTING

What math operation was used to solve each of these problems?

0-7424-1825-1 *Problem Solving*

Name _____ Date _____

Toys, Toys, Toys

1. There are 1,200 toys in a store.

    a. Parents with children under the age of 3 will be able to choose from $\frac{1}{4}$ of the toys. How many toys are for toddlers? Explain.

    b. Parents with children between the ages of 3 and 8 will be able to choose from 30% of the toys. How many toys does the store have for this age group? Explain.

    c. Parents with children between the ages of 9 and 12 will be able to choose from $\frac{2}{5}$ of the toys. What percentage is this? How many toys does the store have for this age group? Explain.

    d. What percentage of the toys are for kids over the age of 12? Explain.

2. A toy maker has 84 wheels.

    a. He uses $\frac{1}{3}$ of the wheels for toy wagons. There are 4 wheels on every wagon. How many wagons will he make? Explain.

    b. He uses $\frac{9}{14}$ of the wheels for toy tricycles. There are 3 wheels on every tricycle. How many tricycles will he make? Explain.

    c. The remainder of the wheels are used for toy scooters. There are 2 wheels on every scooter. How many of these will he make? Explain.

REFLECTING

How are fractions and percentages related?

0-7424-1825-1 *Problem Solving*

Name _____ Date _____

Is It Enough?

Sun-Mi has been saving her money for a new pair of in-line skates. She has saved $85. The skates are regularly priced at $112. The store has them on sale for 20% off.

1. What percentage of the full price will the skates cost?

100% – 20% = _____

2. How much will the skates cost?

_____% × $112 = _____

3. Two days later, the skates are marked 30% off the regular price. How much will the skates cost now? Show your work.

4. There is a 4% sales tax in Sun-Mi's state. How much will the sales tax on the skates be?

0.04 × $_____ = $_____

5. Does Sun-Mi have enough money to buy the skates at 30% off? Explain.

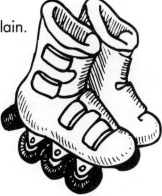

EXPLAINING

Explain how to find the price of a $45 sweater that is on sale for 25% off.

0-7424-1825-1 *Problem Solving*

Name _____ Date _____

Planning a Picnic

The people of Pleasantville celebrate the Fourth of July with a big town picnic. Last year, the following items were served:

25,400 hamburgers
31,500 hot dogs
35,000 ice-cream bars
18,000 pounds of French fries
40,620 cans of soda

This year, the town has grown. The picnic organizers plan to have more food available to cover the added population.

1. They will increase the number of hamburgers by 25%.
How many hamburgers will be needed?

    a. Jody found 25% of 25,400: _____ x _____ = _____

        Then she added that amount to last year's total.

        _____ + 25,400 = _____.

    b. Gordon solved the problem this way.

        100% of the hamburgers we used before + 25% more = 125%

        125% of 25,400 = 1.25 x _____ = _____

    c. Compare the 2 methods. Do they both make sense?
Which do you prefer?

0-7424-1825-1 *Problem Solving*

Name _____ Date _____

Planing a Picnic (cont.)

2. The number of hot dogs will increase by 20%. How many hot dogs will be needed? Explain.

3. The number of ice-cream bars will be doubled. How many ice-cream bars will be needed? Explain.

4. The picnic organizers were short on fries last year. This year they plan to prepare 60% more fries. How many extra pounds of fries will be cooked? Explain.

5. The number of soda cans will be increased by 30%. How many cans will this be in all? Explain.

EXPLAINING

The local soda company puts 48 cans in a case. How many cases will need to be ordered? Explain.

31

Name _____ Date _____

Create Your Own Problems

1. Make up a problem that involves comparing 2 different sets of objects. See if a friend can decide which is more.

2. Choose several numbers larger than 100. Make up questions about the kinds of factors the numbers have. Include at least 2 numbers that are prime.

3. Write a story involving distance, rate, and time. Give 2 pieces of information and see if your friend can find the third.

4. Write 4 questions that involve finding a fraction or percent of a number.

0-7424-1825-1 *Problem Solving*

Name _____ Date _____

Check Your Skills

Answer these questions on a separate piece of paper.

1. Leah found a blouse she liked in 2 different stores. The regular price for the blouse was $75.

Store 1 had the store on sale for 30% off the regular price.
Store 2 had the blouse marked down to 80% of its regular price.

   a. Which store offered the better deal? Explain.

   b. How much money did Leah save? Show your work.

2. Four jets landed at the Kennedy Airport at the same time. Jet 1 carried 460 passengers. Jet 2 carried 10% fewer passengers than jet 1.

   a. How many passengers were on jet 2?

   b. Jet 3 carried 480 passengers. Jet 4 carried $\frac{5}{6}$ as many passengers as jet 3. How many passengers were on jet 4?

   c. How many passengers were on all 4 jets?

3. $7 \times 16 =$ _____

   a. Write an equivalent number sentence using only multiplication.

   b. Write an equivalent number sentence using multiplication and addition.

0-7424-1825-1 *Problem Solving*

Shape Patterns

1. Draw the next three figures in the pattern. Describe the pattern.

2.

a. Describe the pattern in the top row of numbers from one shape to the next.

b. Describe the pattern in the bottom row of numbers from one shape to the next.

c. Describe the pattern between the top and bottom numbers in each shape.

d. Describe the shading pattern.

e. Draw the next 3 figures in the pattern.

EXPANDING

Draw a series of figures that have more than 1 pattern.

0-7424-1825-1 *Problem Solving*

Name _____ Date _____

Function Machine

The function machine uses rules to change numbers.
Look for a pattern in the IN and OUT numbers in each table.
Fill in the table.
Write the rule.

1.

IN	2	4	7	8	9
OUT	10	20	35		

Rule: _____

2.

IN	30	40	45	50	55
OUT	6	8			

Rule: _____

DESCRIBING

Describe how the rules are alike and how the rules are different.

0-7424-1825-1 *Problem Solving*

Name _____ Date _____

Do the Two-Step

This machine uses 2 rules.
Each IN number is changed by 2 rules.
Find the pattern for rule 1.
Then find the pattern for rule 2. Write each rule.

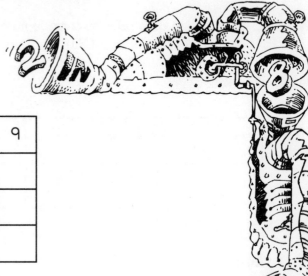

1.

IN	2	3	4	5	6	7	9
OUT	5	6	7				
IN	5	6					
OUT	10	12	14				

Rule 1: _____

Rule 2: _____

2.

IN	3	4	5	6	7	9	10
OUT	9	12	15				
IN	9	12					
OUT	6	9	12				

Rule 1: _____

Rule 2: _____

EXPLAINING

Explain how a 2-step function machine works.

0-7424-1825-1 *Problem Solving*

Number Patterns

Find the patterns in the table.

1. Look at the columns.

   a. Do the columns have a **growing pattern** or a **decreasing pattern**?

   b. Do the columns change at a **steady rate**?

	C1	C2	C3	C4	C5	C6
R1	3	4	7	11	18	
R2	6	8	14	22	36	
R3	12	16	28	44	72	
R4	24	32	56	88	144	

   c. Write the rule for each column.

2. Look at each row.

   a. Do the rows have a **growing pattern** or a **decreasing pattern**?

   b. Do the rows change at a **steady rate**?

   c. Describe the rule for each row.

3. Fill in the sixth column. How do you know you did this correctly?

EXPANDING

Make a table that has a row pattern and a different column pattern.

0-7424-1825-1 *Problem Solving*

Name _____ Date _____

More Number Patterns

Find the patterns in the table.

	C1	C2	C3	C4	C5	C6
R1	20	40	60	80	100	120
R2	18	36	54	72	90	
R3	15	30	45	60	75	
R4	11	22	33	44	55	
R5	6	12	18	24	30	

1. Look at the rows. Describe the rule for the rows.

_____

_____

2. Look at each column.

   a. Do the columns have a **growing pattern** or a **decreasing pattern**?

   b. Do the columns change at a **steady rate**?

   c. Each column has a slightly different pattern. Describe the rule for each column.

   C1:_____   C2: _____

   C3: _____   C4: _____

   C5: _____   C6: _____

   d. Explain the relationship between the patterns from one column to the next.

   e. Fill in the values for column 6. Explain how you did this.

EXPLAINING

Explain how to look for number patterns.

0-7424-1825-1 *Problem Solving*

Name _____ Date _____

Who's Taller?

Danielle, Tamequa, Rashawn, and Joaquín have been good friends since kindergarten. Their heights changed a good deal over the years.

1. When they were in kindergarten, Danielle was taller than Rashawn but not Joaquín. Tamequa was taller than exactly two of the other children.

    a. Put the children in order from shortest to tallest.

    _____ _____ _____ _____
        shortest   tallest

    b. Explain how you found the answer.

2. When they were in third grade, Joaquín was neither the shortest nor the tallest. Rashawn was shorter than Tamequa and Danielle. Danielle was shorter than Tamequa and Joaquín.

Height	1	2	3	4
Danielle				
Tamequa				
Rashawn				
Joaquín				

1 = shortest   4 = tallest

    a. Use the chart. Put an x in a space if the child cannot be that height. Put a circle in the space if the child must be that height.

    b. Put the children in order from shortest to tallest.

    _____ _____ _____ _____
        shortest   tallest

ORGANIZING

Explain the method that helps you organize the clues the best.

                0-7424-1825-1 *Problem Solving*

Name _____ Date _____

All About Order

Danielle, Tamequa, Rashawn, and Joaquín are in Ms. Thompson's fifth-grade class. Use the clues and the logic charts to put the children in order from shortest to tallest and from youngest to oldest.

Clues:
Danielle is not the shortest child.
Rashawn is older than Tamequa and Joaquín.
The shortest child is also the oldest.
Joaquín is taller than exactly one other child.
Danielle is the only child to have the same ranking in both height and age.

Height

	1	2	3	4
Danielle				
Tamequa				
Rashawn				
Joaquín				

1 = shortest   4 = tallest

shortest _____

          _____

          _____

tallest   _____

Age

	1	2	3	4
Danielle				
Tamequa				
Rashawn				
Joaquín				

1 = youngest   4 = oldest

youngest _____

          _____

          _____

oldest   _____

REFLECTING

Danielle is not the shortest. The shortest child is also the oldest.
What do these two clues tell you about Danielle's age?

0-7424-1825-1 *Problem Solving*

Name _____ Date _____

Missing Numbers

Symbols that are the same represent the same number.
Symbols that are different represent different numbers.

1. ♣ × ★ = 16.

    a. Find all the pairs of whole numbers that make the equation true.

      ♣ = _____ ★ = _____   ♣ = _____ ★ = _____

      ♣ = _____ ★ = _____   ♣ = _____ ★ = _____

    b. How do you know you found all possibilities?

    c. What is a name that describes all the numbers you found in part **a**? _____

2. ♦ ÷ ♥ = 6. Find at least 4 pairs of whole numbers that make the equation true.

    ♦ = _____   ♥ = _____

    ♦ = _____   ♥ = _____

    ♦ = _____   ♥ = _____

    ♦ = _____   ♥ = _____

REFLECTING

Is it possible to find all possible whole numbers that make the equation
in problem 2 true? Why or why not?

0-7424-1825-1 *Problem Solving*

Name _____ Date _____

Missing Numbers

Symbols that are the same represent the same number.
Symbols that are different represent different numbers.

1. ♣ + ♣ + ♣ = 27   ♣ = _____

2. ♦ + ♦ = 26   ♦ = _____

3. Is there more than one possible answer for ♣?
   For ♦? Explain.

4. ★ − ★ = ♥

   ★ = _____   ♥ = _____

5. ☺ ÷ ☺ = ✿

   ☺ = _____   ✿ = _____

EXPANDING

Try different values for ★. What do you notice about the value of ♥?

Try different values for ☺. What do you notice about the value of ✿?

0-7424-1825-1 *Problem Solving*

Name _____ Date _____

Missing Numbers

Find the value of each shape.

1. $7 \times \hexagon = 35$ $\hexagon$ = _____

2. $15 \times 60 = \blacksquare \times 9$ $\blacksquare$ = _____

3. $17 \times \bullet = 34 \times 2$ $\bullet$ = _____

4. $\triangle \div 45 = 38 \div 19$ $\triangle$ = _____

5. $80 \div 20 = 16 - \pentagon$ $\pentagon$ = _____

6. Find the numbers that make all 3 equations true. Shapes that are the same represent the same number. Shapes that are different represent different numbers.

    $\triangle + \triangle + \triangle = 15$ $\triangle$ = _____

    $\triangle + \hexagon + \trapezoid = 15$ $\hexagon$ = _____

    $\triangle + \trapezoid = 9$ $\trapezoid$ = _____

EXPLAINING

Explain the strategies you used to find your answers.

0-7424-1825-1 *Problem Solving*

Finding Unknowns

The fifth-grade classes voted on the location of their class trip. They could choose the beach, the amusement park, or the science museum.

B = beach   **A** = amusement park   **S** = science museum

Room 9:

12 votes for the beach

5 votes for the science museum

27 votes in all

B = _____   **A** = _____   **S** = _____

Room 10:

10 votes for the beach

3 times more votes for the amusement park than for the science museum

30 votes in all

B = _____   **A** = _____   **S** = _____

Room 11:

4 votes for the science museum

8 votes for the beach

$\frac{1}{2}$ as many votes for the beach as for the amusement park

_____ votes in all

B = _____   **A** = _____   **S** = _____

EXPLAINING

Explain the strategies you used to find your answers.

0-7424-1825-1 *Problem Solving*

Making Equations

A box has a square base with a side length of 6 inches.

1. What if the box had a height of 8 inches?

a. How many 1-inch cubes would fit along the bottom of the box? _____

b. How many layers of cubes would fit in the box? _____

c. How many total cubes fit inside the box? Show your work.

d. What measurement did you just find? _____

2. How many cubes would fit inside a box that is 5 inches high? Show your work.

3. How many cubes would fit inside a box that is 10 inches high? Show your work.

4. Let **H** be the height of the box. Write an equation that shows how to find the number of cubes, **C**, that would fit inside the box.

C = _____

8 in.

6 in.

EXPANDING

A box has a square base with a side length of 4 inches. Let **H** be the height of the box. Write an equation that shows how to find the number of cubes, **C**, that would fit inside the box.

0-7424-1825-1 *Problem Solving*

Name _____ Date _____

Making Equations

1. Sandra gets a job baby-sitting for the Andersons. They pay her $4 per hour.

    a. How much will she make if she baby-sits for 3 hours? _____

    b. How much will she make if she baby-sits for 4 hours? _____

    c. Let **H** be the number of hours she works. Let **M** be the amount of money she makes. Write an equation.

        M = _____

2. Uyen's father is taking her and some friends to the movies for her birthday. Movie tickets cost $5 per child and $8 per adult.

    a. Uyen brings 4 friends. How much will the children's tickets cost?

    b. What will be the total cost of all the tickets (including Uyen's father)?

    c. What will be the total cost of all the tickets if Uyen brings 6 friends? Show your work.

    d. Let **T** be the number of children's tickets. Let **C** be the total cost of all the tickets.

        Write an equation. **C** = _____

DESCRIBING

Music lessons cost $10 per lesson. Let **L** be the number of lessons. Let **C** be the total cost. Write an equation. Describe the process you used to find the equation.

    C = _____

46

Tall Towers

Materials: cubes

> **Surface area** is the sum of the areas of each face.

Use cubes to build the towers. Then answer the questions.

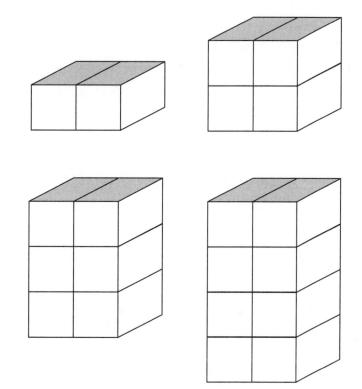

1. Complete the table.

Height of Tower: (units)	1	2	3	4	5
Surface Area: (square units)					

2. Build a tower that is 5 units high. What is the surface area of this tower? Add this value to your table.

0-7424-1825-1 *Problem Solving*

Name _____ Date _____

Tall Towers (cont.)

3. What happens each time you add another layer to the tower?

4. What is the surface area of a tower that is 10 units tall? Explain.

5. Write a sentence describing how to find the total surface area for any height.

6. Let **H** be the height of the tower. Let **S** be the total surface area. Write an equation.

S = _____

REFLECTING

How does building a model, making a table, and describing the process in words help you make an equation for the surface area?

48

Name _____ Date _____

Show Me the Money!

Sara is 11 years old. Sara's grandmother offered to help pay for college. Her grandmother gave her two options.

Option 1: $1,000 each year on her birthday, ending on her eighteenth birthday.

Option 2: $100 on her twelfth birthday. Each birthday after that will be double the previous year's amount, ending on her eighteenth birthday.

1. Complete the table for option 1.

Birthday	12	13	14	15	16	17	18
Total Amt. Saved	1,000						

2. How much total money will Sara have saved for college after her eighteenth birthday? _____

3. Describe the pattern in the table. How does Sara's fund grow?

0-7424-1825-1 *Problem Solving*

Show Me the Money! (cont.)

4. Complete the table for option 2.

Birthday	12	13	14	15	16	17	18
Amt. Rcvd. Each Birthday	100	200					
Total Amt. Saved	100	300					

5. How much money will Sara have saved for college after her eighteenth birthday? _____

6. Describe the pattern in the table. How does Sara's fund grow?

7. Which option should Sara choose? Why?

8. Should Sara's choice be different if the plan ends after her sixteenth birthday? Explain.

COMPARING

Make a scatterplot for each option. Write a description comparing the graphs. What is different about how the savings grow? Does the amount of time the plan is in place make a difference in which option should be chosen?

 0-7424-1825-1 *Problem Solving*

Name _____ Date _____

Growing Patterns

Materials: tiles or cubes

Use tiles or cubes to make these shapes. Look for a pattern.
Use the pattern to draw the next shape.

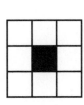 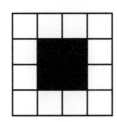 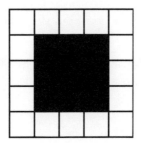

1. Describe the pattern.

2. Make a table.

Shape	1st	2nd	3rd	4th	5th
Number of Tiles	8	12	16		

3. How many tiles in the 10th shape? _____ The 15th? _____

DESCRIBING

Describe how the pattern grows. Be specific.

0-7424-1825-1 *Problem Solving*

Create Your Own Problems

1. Make a function machine. Decide on a rule. Make a table of IN and OUT values. See if a classmate can find the rule.

2. Make a table with 2 different number patterns, one type of pattern for the rows and another type for the columns.

3. Gary, Denise, Enrique, and Lucia are standing in line at the movies. Decide what order they are standing in. Make up 3 to 4 clues that will help someone find their order. Try not to make the clues too obvious, but make sure there is enough information to find the correct order. Give your clues to a classmate. Check your classmate's answer. Does it match yours? If not, does it fit all the clues? If it doesn't match but does fit all your clues, then try including another clue that eliminates your classmate's answer. Try your new set of clues on another classmate.

4. Make up 4 equations that have missing numbers. Pick a symbol or shape to represent the missing number. Give your equations to a classmate to solve.

0-7424-1825-1 *Problem Solving*

Name _____ Date _____

Check Your Skills

Answer these questions on a separate piece of paper.

1. Complete the table. Find the rule for the function machine.

IN	2	4	5	7	11	12
OUT	8	16	20			

Rule: _____

2. Find the missing numbers.

   a. ◆ x 7 = 3 x 21

   b. 75 ÷ 15 = 35 ÷ ♣

3. Gary, Lisa, Allyson, and Becky are all in the same class. Becky is neither the shortest nor the tallest. Gary is shorter than Allyson. Lisa is taller than only one of the other children. Put the children in order from shortest to tallest.

4. Tickets to a minor league baseball game cost $6 each.

   a. How much will 5 tickets cost? _____

   b. How much will 12 tickets cost? _____

   c. Let **T** be the number of tickets. Let **C** be the total cost. Write an equation.

      C = _____

5. Complete these number patterns and write the rule.

   a. 4 9 13 22 ____ ____ ____ ____

      Rule: _____

   b. 37,500 7,500 1,500 _____ _____ _____

      Rule: _____

   c. 4 12 36 ____ ____ ____ ____

      Rule: _____

0-7424-1825-1 *Problem Solving*

Name _____ Date _____

A Class by Itself

Materials: a ruler and a protractor

Classifying Triangles by Side Lengths	Classifying Triangles by Angle Measurements
An **equilateral** triangle has 3 equal sides. An **isosceles** triangle has 2 equal sides. A **scalene** triangle has no equal sides.	A **right** triangle has one 90° angle. All the angles of an **acute** triangle are less than 90°. An **obtuse** triangle has one angle measure greater than 90°.

I. Measure the sides of each triangle. Write **equilateral**, **isosceles**, or **scalene** on the first line. Measure the angles of each triangle. Write **acute**, **obtuse**, or **right** on the second line.

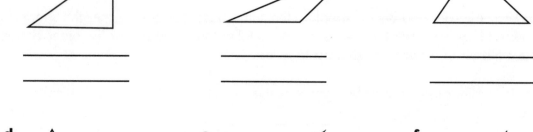

a.

_____
_____

b.

_____
_____

c.

_____
_____

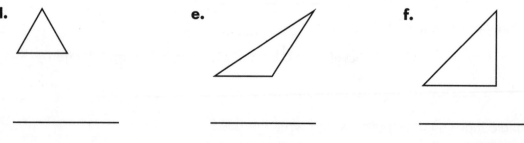

d.

_____
_____

e.

_____
_____

f.

_____
_____

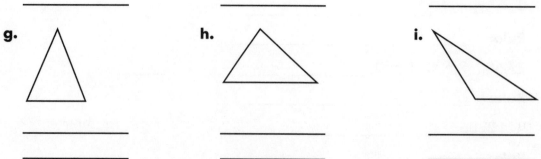

g.

_____
_____

h.

_____
_____

i.

_____
_____

0-7424-1825-1 *Problem Solving*

Name _____ Date _____

A Class by Itself (cont.)

2. Look at the triangles on the previous page. Decide where each triangle should fit on the chart. Write its letter in the correct space. Then answer the questions.

	obtuse	acute	right
scalene			
equilateral			
isosceles			

a. Which spaces on the chart are empty?

b. Try to draw a triangle to match the empty categories. What do you notice?

c. What can you say about the angle measurements of an equilateral triangle?

EXPLAINING

Explain why triangles are classified by side lengths and angle measurements.

Name _____ Date _____

Pondering Polygons

These shapes are **polygons**.	These shapes are **not polygons**.
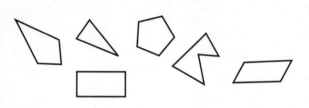	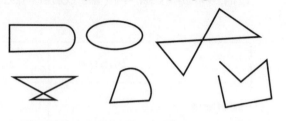

1. Make a list of characteristics that define a polygon.

2. Test each polygon against the list. Each polygon should have all the characteristics. If one does not fit, then the list is too specific. Modify the list.

3. Test each non-polygon against the list. Each of these shapes should lack one of the characteristics. If any non-polygon matches all the characteristics, then the list is too general. Modify the list.

4. Is each characteristic necessary? Check to see if any of the characteristics can be eliminated. Would all the polygons still fit? Would all the non-polygons still be excluded? Modify the list.

DESCRIBING

How can you tell whether or not a shape is a polygon? Describe your process.

0-7424-1825-1 *Problem Solving*

Name _____ Date _____

Parallelograms

Polygons with 4 sides are called **quadrilaterals**.
Quadrilaterals can be divided into 2 groups.

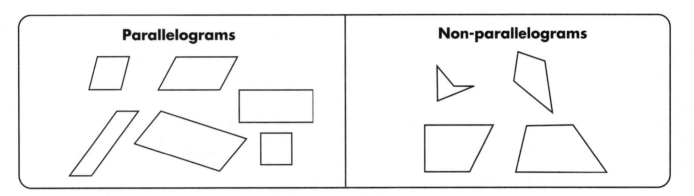

| Parallelograms | Non-parallelograms |

1. Make a list of characteristics that define a parallelogram. One characteristic is given.

   a quadrilateral

2. Test each parallelogram against the list. Each parallelogram should have all the characteristics. If one does not fit, then the list is too specific. Modify the list.

3. Test each non-parallelogram against the list. Each of these shapes should lack one of the characteristics. If any non-parallelogram matches all the characteristics, then the list is too general. Modify the list.

4. Is each characteristic necessary? Check to see if any of the characteristics can be eliminated. Would all the parallelograms still fit? Would all the non-parallelograms still be excluded? Modify the list.

EXPLAINING

Explain how to create a good definition by looking at examples and non-examples.

0-7424-1825-1 *Problem Solving*

Name _____ Date _____

Quadrilaterals

Put each of the following words into its place on the organizational chart: **square**, **kite**, **parallelogram**, **trapezoid**, **rectangle**, **rhombus**, **other**, and **non-parallelogram**. Draw an example of the shape next to each word in the chart.

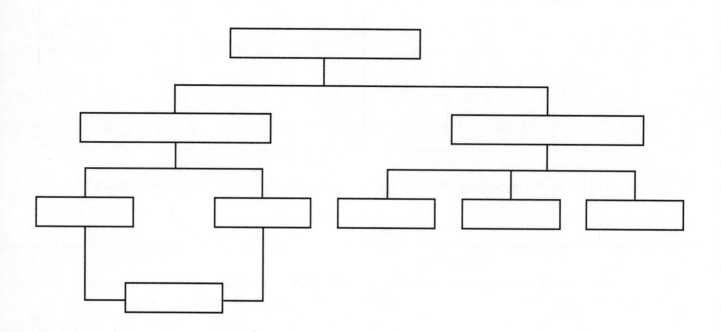

Write **true** or **false** next to each statement.

1. All parallelograms are rectangles. _____

2. All rectangles are parallelograms. _____

3. All rhombi are squares. _____

4. All rhombi are rectangles. _____

5. All squares are rhombi. _____

6. Some kites are parallelograms. _____

7. Some trapezoids are kites. _____

8. All squares are rectangles. _____

0-7424-1825-1 *Problem Solving*

Name _____ Date _____

Angle Sums

> A **diagonal** connects 2 non-adjacent vertices.

1. Name this polygon.

2. Draw diagonals to divide the shape into triangles.

    a. How many triangles were formed? _____

    b. What is the angle sum of any triangle? _____

    c. What happens if you add all angles in the triangles together?

    d. What is the angle sum of the shape? _____

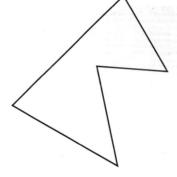

3. Name this polygon.

4. Draw diagonals to divide the shape into triangles.

    a. How many triangles were formed? _____

    b. What is the angle sum of the shape? Explain.

5. What do the polygons in problems 1 and 3 have in common? Draw 2 more polygons like these. Draw diagonals to divide the shapes into triangles. What do you notice?

REFLECTING

Write a statement that is true for any pentagon.

0-7424-1825-1 *Problem Solving*

Name _____ Date _____

Angle Sums

Draw diagonals to divide each polygon into triangles. Calculate the angle sum of each polygon. Complete the table. Answer the questions.

Number of Sides	Number of Triangles	Angle Sum
3	1	180°
4		
5		
6		
7		
8		
9		

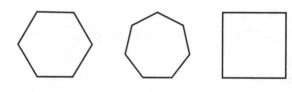

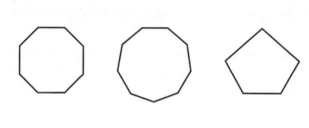

1. What is the relationship between the number of triangles **t** and the number of sides **n**? Describe it in words. Then write an equation.

2. What is the relationship between the angle sum **S** and the number of triangles **t**? Describe it in words. Then write an equation.

EXPLAINING

How can you find the angle sum of any polygon? Write an equation relating the angle sum **S** and the number of sides **n**.

60

Name _____ Date _____

Prisms and Pyramids

Many three-dimensional shapes fit into two categories: **prisms** and **pyramids**. Examples of prisms and pyramids are given below. The shaded portions of each shape are called **bases**. The other sides are called **faces**.

prisms	pyramids

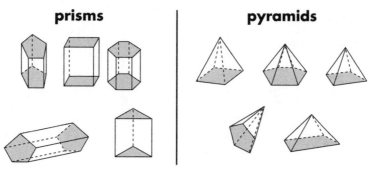

1. Examine the prisms and pyramids. Look for similarities and differences. Make a list of characteristics that define each category.

    Prism Characteristics   **Pyramid Characteristics**

2. Modify each list. Make the list as short as possible, using only the necessary characteristics.

EXPLAINING

Explain how you chose the characteristics.

0-7424-1825-1 *Problem Solving*

Name _____ Date _____

Plotting Pleasantville

The grid lines on the map represent streets. Each grid square is a block.

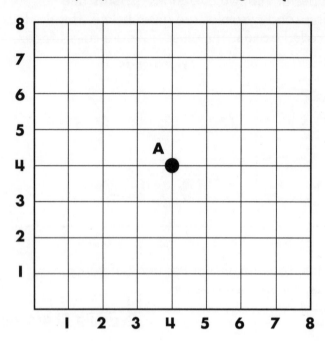

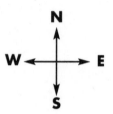

1. Plot a point for each building in Pleasantville. Label the point with the corresponding letter. The first one has been done for you.

   a. The town hall is located at (4, 4).

   b. The library is 3 blocks east and 2 blocks north of the town hall.

   c. The school is 3 blocks south and 2 blocks west of the town hall.

   d. The shopping center is 6 blocks west and 1 block south of the library.

   e. The police station is 7 blocks east and 3 blocks south of the shopping center.

   f. The Lakeside Apartments are located at (6, 8).

0-7424-1825-1 *Problem Solving*

Name _____ Date _____

Plotting Pleasantville (cont.)

2. Describe the shortest route between each pair of buildings. You must stay on the streets.

a. town hall and police station

b. school and Lakeside Apartments

c. shopping center and police station

d. town hall and library

3. How many blocks will you walk for each route in problem 2?

a. _____   **b.** _____

c. _____   **d.** _____

4. Write the coordinates of each point.

a. library (_____, _____)   **b.** school (_____, _____)

c. shopping (_____, _____)   **d.** police (_____, _____)

EXPANDING

Make a map of a town of your invention. Write clues for the location of the buildings. Ask a friend to plot the buildings on the map.

0-7424-1825-1 *Problem Solving*

Name _____ Date _____

Finding Routes

How far do the students of Orchard Grove Elementary have to travel to get to school? Look at the map. The grid lines are streets. Each grid square is a block. The letters show where the students (Emily, Jalisa, Karam, Lauren, Melika, Raul, Steve, and Tia) live.

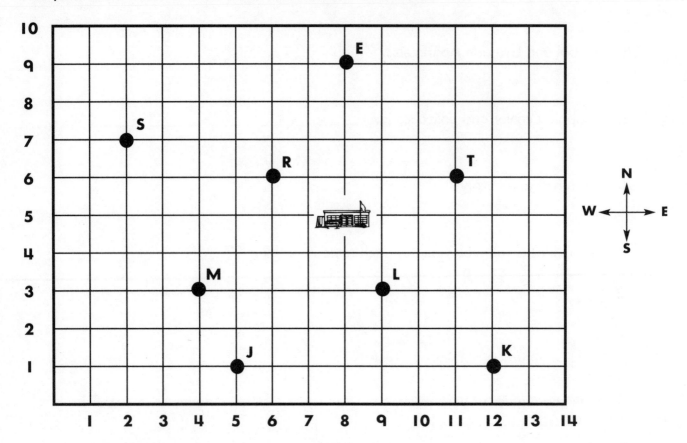

1. Write the map coordinates of each student's house.

    a. Emily _(8, 9)_   **b.** Jalisa _____   **c.** Karam _____

    d. Lauren _____   **e.** Melika _____   **f.** Raul _____

    g. Steve _____   **h.** Tia _____

2. Which student travels 2 blocks north and 4 blocks east to get to school? _____

0-7424-1825-1 *Problem Solving*

Name _____ Date _____

Finding Routes (cont.)

3. Steve's father drives Steve and his cousin to school. From Steve's house, they travel 6 blocks south and 3 blocks east to his cousin's house.

a. Who is Steve's cousin? _____

b. Describe the route from the cousin's house to school.

4. Find the shortest distance each student travels to get to school.

a. Emily _____   **b.** Jalisa _____   **c.** Karam _____

d. Lauren _____   **e.** Melika _____   **f.** Raul _____

g. Steve _____   **h.** Tia _____

5. Students who live within 5 blocks from the school must walk. Which students walk to school?

DESCRIBING

Lauren's mother is picking up Emily, Melika, Jalisa, and Tia for a trip to the movies. The theater is located at the point (1, 2) on the map. In what order should they pick up the other girls? Describe the best route. How far will they travel?

0-7424-1825-1 *Problem Solving*

Name _____ Date _____

Line Symmetry

Materials: tracing paper

A figure has **line symmetry** when a line can be drawn to create 2 identical mirror-image halves. Some shapes have more than 1 line of symmetry. A square has 4 lines of symmetry.

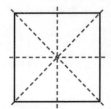

Trace each shape onto a small square of tracing paper. Fold each shape in half different ways. If the halves match, then the folded crease is a line of symmetry. Draw dotted lines on the shapes to show all lines of symmetry. If the shape does not have any lines of symmetry, write **none** below the shape.

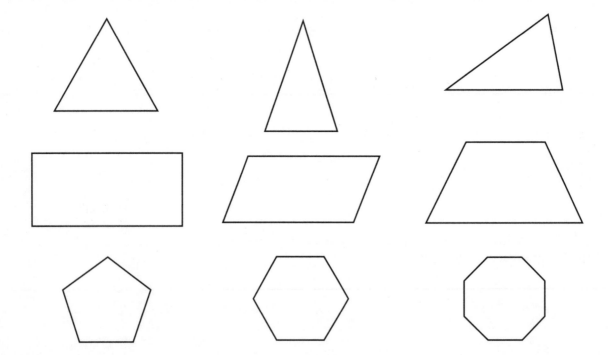

EXPANDING

A **regular polygon** has sides that are all the same length. Find the equilateral triangle, the square, the regular pentagon, and the regular hexagon in the shapes above. Write a statement about regular polygons and lines of symmetry.

66

   0-7424-1825-1 *Problem Solving*

Name _____ Date _____

Reflections

Draw the **reflection** of each figure across the line.

1.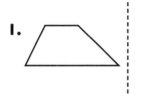

2.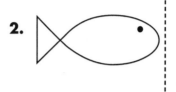

3.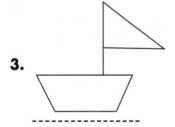

4.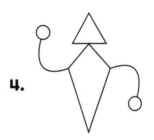

5. How does the size and shape of each image compare to that of its reflection?

COMPARING

How are reflections and line symmetry related?

0-7424-1825-1 *Problem Solving*

Name _____ Date _____

Rotations

Draw each shape after it has been **rotated** around the point.

1. 90° clockwise

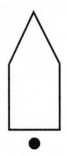

2. 180°

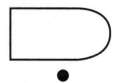

3. 90° counterclockwise

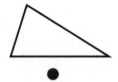

4. 90° counterclockwise

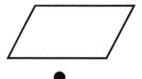

COMPARING

 How does the size and shape of each image compare with that of its rotation?

0-7424-1825-1 *Problem Solving*

Translations

For each translation, write the coordinates of the image. Draw the translation on the coordinate grid. Write the coordinates of each translation point.

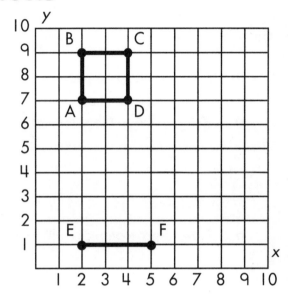

1. Translate ABCD 4 units to the right.

	Image	Translation
A	(2, 7)	
B		
C		
D		

2. Translate ABCD 2 units to the right and 3 units down.

	Image	Translation
A	(2, 7)	
B		
C		
D		

3. Translate $\overline{EF}$ 3 units to the right.

	Image	Translation
E	(2, 1)	
F		

4. Explain how translations of the square and segment were used to create a picture.

EXPANDING

How did the coordinates change for each type of translation? If the point (x, y) is translated 4 units to the right, what will happen to the values of x and y?

0-7424-1825-1 *Problem Solving*

Name _____ Date _____

Toothpick Troubles

Materials: toothpicks

1. Use toothpicks to make squares.

    a. What is the smallest number of toothpicks needed to make a square? Draw a picture.

    b. How many toothpicks will be used to make the next smallest square? Draw a picture.

2. Arrange 7 toothpicks to make 3 triangles. Draw a picture.

3. Arrange 8 toothpicks to make 8 triangles (toothpicks may overlap). Draw a picture.

EXPANDING

 Arrange a set of toothpicks so they make shapes. Write a problem challenging a friend to make the same number of shapes using that many toothpicks.

     0-7424-1825-1 *Problem Solving*

Name _____ Date _____

Mosaic Madness

Materials: pattern blocks or pattern-block templates (pages 108–109)

The Pleasantville town council wants to design a tile floor for the entrance of the town hall. They want an eye-catching geometric pattern.

1. Use 2 to 3 different shapes from the pattern block templates. Color and cut out the templates. Create a **tiling pattern** (the shapes fit together without any gaps or overlaps). Draw your tiling pattern.

2. Use different shapes to create another tiling pattern. Draw your tiling pattern.

REFLECTING

Pattern blocks are created so that many different tiling patterns are possible. How did the designers know how to make the blocks so they all fit together?

0-7424-1825-1 *Problem Solving*

Name _____ Date _____

Tiling Patterns

1. A **tiling pattern** occurs when shapes fit together around a single point without any gaps or overlaps. This is an example of a tiling pattern.

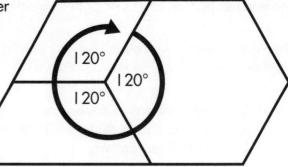

    a. Find the sum of the angle measurements around the point.

    b. Why does this angle sum make sense for a tiling pattern?

2. These 2 triangles, the square, and the rhombus do not make a tiling pattern.

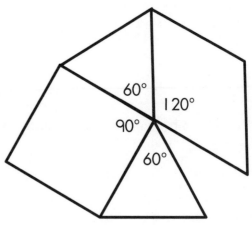

    a. Why doesn't this diagram fit the definition of a tiling pattern?

    b. Find the sum of the angle measurements around the point. How could you tell from the angle sum that these shapes would not tile?

    c. Write a true statement about tiling patterns and angle sums around a point.

EXPANDING

Could you make this a tiling pattern by adding one more shape? What shape would you add? What would have to be the measure of one of its angles?

0-7424-1825-1 *Problem Solving*

Name _____ Date _____

To Tile or Not to Tile

Materials: protractor, pattern blocks or pattern-block templates (pages 108–109)

> All the sides and all the angles of a **regular polygon** are congruent.
>
> A **tiling pattern** occurs when shapes fit together around a single point without gaps or overlaps.

1. Is a square a regular polygon? Why or why not?

2. Cut out the square templates on page 109. See if you can put them together to create a **tiling pattern**.

a. Can a tiling pattern be created from only squares? _____

b. How many squares fit around a single point? _____

c. What is the measure of one angle of a square? _____

d. To create a tiling pattern, the angle sum around a point must be _____ .

e. How are your answers to parts a–d related?

0-7424-1825-1 *Problem Solving*

To Tile or Not to Tile (cont.)

3. Look at the hexagon templates from page 108.

a. Is this a **regular hexagon**? Why or why not?

b. Use a protractor to measure an angle of the hexagon template.

each angle = _____ degrees

c. Can you create a tiling pattern using only hexagons? If so, how many hexagons would be needed? Explain how the angle measure helped you answer these questions.

d. Test your answer to part c by cutting out the hexagon templates and putting them together to see if they tile.

4. Pentagons are not found in a set of pattern blocks.

a. Why do you think this is true?

b. Each angle of a regular pentagon measures 108°. Can a tiling pattern be created using only pentagons? Explain.

EXPLAINING

Explain how knowing the angle measure of a regular polygon can help you decide whether or not a tiling pattern can be created using only that shape.

0-7424-1825-1 *Problem Solving*

Name _____ Date _____

Timely Tiling

Materials: pattern blocks or pattern-block templates (pages 108–109)

Timely Tiling creates and installs custom-designed tiling patterns for floors, walls, and countertops.

1. Mr. Franklin wants to design a kitchen floor using regular hexagons and equilateral triangles.

    a. What is the measure of each angle in an equilateral triangle? How do you know?

    b. Each angle of a regular hexagon measures 120°. Can you create a tiling pattern using regular hexagons and equilateral triangles? If so, how many of each would you use?

    c. Use the hexagon and triangle pattern-block templates from pages 108 and 109. Design a tiling pattern for Mr. Franklin.

    d. Extend the tiling pattern you created to show how it will look on Mr. Franklin's rectangular floor. Draw and color the pattern.

2. Mr. Gilbert wants a countertop pattern design. He wants a design that includes only regular pentagons and regular hexagons. Explain to Mr. Gilbert why his demands are impossible. (Each angle in a regular pentagon measures 108°.)

EXPANDING

Be creative. Come up with 2 new designs for Timely Tiling. Include specific instructions to the designers detailing side lengths and angle measurements of each shape used. Include a color drawing of your tiling pattern.

     0-7424-1825-1 *Problem Solving*

Name _____ Date _____

Create Your Own Problems

1. Draw 6 different triangles. Make each triangle a different type. Ask a classmate to name your triangles using both angle measurement and side length characteristics.

2. Ask 4 questions that test understanding of parallelogram characteristics.

3. Write 6 true and false questions about different types of quadrilaterals.

4. Choose 3 different polygons. Ask questions about the angle sums.

5. Make a map on a coordinate grid. Ask questions about routes and distances between places on your map.

6. Ask 4 questions about whether or not certain combinations of polygons create tiling patterns.

0-7424-1825-1 *Problem Solving*

Name _____ Date _____

Check Your Skills

Answer the following questions on a separate piece of paper.

1. Name the following triangles based on angle measurement and side length characteristics.

   a.    **b.**   **c.**

2. Why is there no such thing as an obtuse equilateral triangle?

3. Find the sum of all the angles in a heptagon. Show your work.

4. Explain the differences between prisms and pyramids.

5. Will each combination of shapes create a tiling pattern? If so, how many of each shape will be needed? Explain how you know.

   a. squares and equilateral triangles

   b. regular octagons (each angle is 135°)

   c. regular hexagons (each angle is 120°), squares, and parallelograms with angle measures of 150° and 30°.

0-7424-1825-1 *Problem Solving*

Name _____   Date _____

Estimating Will Do

Materials: centimeter ruler, dollar-bill templates (see page 110)

How many dollar bills would it take to cover your desk?

1. **Estimate.** _____

2. **Calculate.**

   a. Use a centimeter ruler to measure the dimensions of a dollar bill.

      width = _____ cm   length = _____ cm

   b. How much space does a dollar bill cover? _____

   c. What type of measurement is this? _____

   d. Use a meter stick to measure the dimensions of your desk.

      width = _____ cm   length = _____ cm

   e. How much space does your desk top cover? _____

   f. What type of measurement is this? _____

   g. How many dollar bills will fit on your desk? Explain how you found your answer.

0-7424-1825-1 *Problem Solving*

Name _____ Date _____

Estimating Will Do (cont.)

3. **Test.** Cut out the dollar bill templates. Lay them edge to edge on top of your desk. How many dollar bills fit? If any bills hang over the edge of the desk, you will have to estimate fractional parts of bills.

4. **Compare**. How do your estimate, test answer, and calculation compare? Which is most accurate? Least accurate?

5. Find a table that has a larger surface than your desk. How many dollar bills would it take to cover the table?

    a. Estimate. _____

    b. Calculate. _____
       Show your work.

    c. Test. _____

6. Calculate how many dollar bills it would take to cover the floor of your classroom. Show your work.

REFLECTING

Is it practical to test your calculation for problem 6, or can you rely on your calculation?

0-7424-1825-1 *Problem Solving*

Name _____ Date _____

Fencing In

1. Toby has 2 new puppies. The fence around the perimeter of their rectangular yard needs to be replaced to keep the puppies safe.

   a. The property is 50 ft. wide by 120 ft. long. How much fencing will Toby need? Show your work.

   b. Fencing panels come in 6 ft. or 5 ft. lengths. Both lengths cost the same per foot. Which size would you order? Why?

   c. How many fence panels will you need? Show your work.

2. Mrs. Potter is making a vegetable garden shaped like the one shown here. How much fencing will she need to go all around the garden? Show your work.

5 m   3 m

4 m

3. Farmer Hanson's property has an irregular shape. How much fencing will he need to enclose the entire property? Show your work.

50 ft.   50 ft.

100 ft.

450 ft.

REFLECTING

What type of measurement did you find in each of these problems?

80

Name _____ Date _____

Rectangular Reasoning

The Hernandez family bought 32 ft. of fencing to surround a rectangular garden.

1. Give possible dimensions of the garden.

    a. length = _____ ft.   **b.** width = _____ ft.

2. Explain how you found your answer.

3. Find other dimensions that will give the same perimeter.

    a. length = _____ ft.   **b.** width = _____ ft.

4. Complete the following equation for the rectangular garden with a perimeter of 32 ft.

length + width = _____ ft.

5. The perimeter of a rectangular garden is 40 ft. Complete the following equation.

length + width = _____ ft.

6. The perimeter of a rectangular garden is **P.** Complete the following equation.

length + width = _____

      0-7424-1825-1 *Problem Solving*

Rectangular Reasoning (cont.)

7. Find the area of the garden that has the dimensions you chose in problem 1.

8. Could the garden have dimensions that would give it a larger area? Explain.

9. The dimensions of the garden must be whole numbers. Make a table of all possible garden dimensions with a perimeter of 32 ft. Then find the area of each garden.

length	1														
width	15														
area	15														

10. What dimensions give you the garden with the largest area?

    a. length = _____ ft.   **b.** width = _____ ft.

REFLECTING

What type of rectangle gave you the largest area for a perimeter of 32 ft.? Do you think this will be true for any perimeter? Make tables for rectangular gardens with perimeters of 20 ft. and 40 ft. to check your answer.

82

Name _____ Date _____

Confounding Confetti

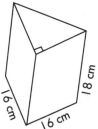

Materials: graph paper

A party-supplies manufacturer created a unique box to package its Confounding Confetti. The top and bottom of the box are shaped like right triangles. The sides of the box are rectangles.

1. Make a copy of the bottom of the box. Use a piece of graph paper. Each grid square represents 1 square centimeter. Draw a right triangle with legs 16 cm in length.

    a. How much confetti will fit along the bottom of the box? _____ Count grid squares to get your answer.

    b. Use a formula to calculate the amount of confetti that will fit along the bottom of the box. Show your work.

    c. What type of measurement is this? _____

2. Find out how much confetti will fit inside the box.

    a. How many 1-cm-tall layers of confetti will fit in the box? _____

    b. How much confetti will a full box hold? Show your work.

    c. What type of measurement is this? _____

EXPLAINING

Explain how to find the volume of a box with a triangular base. What do you need to know?

0-7424-1825-1 *Problem Solving*

Name _____ Date _____

Calling All Units

I cm   = ——

I inch = ——————

1. Compare the lengths of the lines above. About how many centimeters make up I inch? Describe the strategy you used to get your answer.

2. Mr. Hanson's fifth-grade class took the following measurements, but they forgot to write down the units. Some of the students measured in inches and some in centimeters. Help them figure out which measurements were taken in inches and which in centimeters.

Object	Measurement	Units
binder length	8.5	
binder width	28	
desk top width	60	
desk top length	18	
desk height	36	
door width	30	
door height	210	

3. Mr. Hanson says all the measurements should be recorded in inches. There isn't time to take the measurements again. Use your answer from problem I to find each object's measurement in inches.

DESCRIBING

Describe the strategies you used to solve problems 2 and 3.

0-7424-1825-1 *Problem Solving*

Name _____ Date _____

A Matter of Time

1. How many hours are in 1 week? Show your work.

2. How much time do you spend at school in a week? Show your work.

3. How much time do you spend sleeping in a week? A year? Show your work.

4. How much time do you spend doing other things besides going to school and sleeping in a week? Show your work.

5. What percent of your week do you spend in school? Sleeping? Doing other things? Explain how you got your answers.

REFLECTING

What did you need to know to solve these problems?

85

Name _____ Date _____

The Temperature Is Rising

The formulas give good estimates for temperatures between 32 and 95 degrees Fahrenheit.

> **Formula:** To convert Celsius temperatures to Fahrenheit temperatures, multiply the Celsius temperature by 1.8 and then add 30.
>
> **Reverse Formula:** To convert Fahrenheit temperatures to Celsius, _____ 30 and _____ by 1.8.

1. The temperature is 48 degrees Fahrenheit. What is the temperature in Celsius? Show your work.

2. The temperature in the room is 25 degrees Celsius. What is the temperature in degrees Fahrenheit? Show your work.

3. The temperature outside is 35 degrees Celsius. Would you be more likely to go swimming or skiing? Explain your answer.

4. It is a hot day in July. You estimate the Celsius temperature to be _____. Explain how you reached your estimate.

REFLECTING

When is it important to know the exact temperature?

0-7424-1825-1 *Problem Solving*

Name _____ Date _____

Weighty Matters

> 1 kilogram (kg) = 2.2 pounds (lb.)
>
> 1 ton (T.) = 2,000 pounds

1. The giant panda eats about 60 lbs. of bamboo a day. How many kilograms is this? Show your work.

2. The heaviest flying bird is a Kori from Africa. It can weigh as much as 11 kg. How many pounds is this? Show your work.

3. A tractor trailer weighs 3 T. How many kilograms is this? Show your work.

4. A very large killer whale weighs 8,000 kg. How many tons is this? Show your work.

EXPLAINING

Explain how to convert from pounds to kilograms. Explain how to convert from kilograms to pounds.

0-7424-1825-1 *Problem Solving*

Name _____ Date _____

Lively Liquids

> 1 gallon = 3.8 liters
>
> 1 gallon = 4 quarts
>
> 1 quart = 2 pints

1. Loni's family went through 2 gallons of milk this week. How many liters is this? Show your work.

2. Mrs. Taylor's car uses 200 liters of gas a week. How many gallons of gas is this? Show your work.

3. The school cafeteria serves juice in 1-pint containers. They sell 1,656 pints in a week. How many liters of juice are served in a week? Show your work.

REFLECTING

Which problems required more than one step? How can you tell when more than one calculation is required?

0-7424-1825-1 *Problem Solving*

The Better Buy

1. A bag of 24 apples $3.00. The same type of apples can be bought for $0.15 per apple. Which is the better buy? Explain.

2. Carpet cleaner comes in two sizes: 24 oz. for $3.08 or 36 oz. for $4.99. Which is the better buy? Explain.

3. Jamal is buying a group of solar power panels. He knows that a minimum of 3,456 square inches of panels are needed for generating the power he needs. The panels come in two sizes: 18 inches by 30 inches or 24 inches by 36 inches.

    a. If he buys the smaller panels, how many will he need? Explain.

    b. If he buys the larger panels, how many will he need? Explain.

    c. The smaller panels cost $42.89 each, and the larger panels cost $86.90 each. Which size offers the better buy? Explain.

    d. How much will the panels cost? Explain.

EXPLAINING

Explain how to find the better buy for 2 items of different sizes.

0-7424-1825-1 *Problem Solving*

Name _____ Date _____

Create Your Own Problems

1. Make up 3 problems relating the area of common objects to the area of post-it notes.

2. Draw a picture representing a farmer's field. Make the field an irregular shape. Ask questions about the perimeter of the field.

3. Draw a picture of a container. Ask questions to help someone find out how much it will hold.

4. Make up 4 questions about temperature.

5. Make up 2 questions about finding the better buy between 2 items of different sizes.

6. Make up 4 questions that involve converting units of capacity and weight.

0-7424-1825-1 *Problem Solving*

Name _____ Date _____

Check Your Skills

Answer these questions on a separate piece of paper.

1. How many 4" x 6" index cards will fit on the surface of a 2' by 3' table? Show your work.

2. The Nicholson family bought 64 ft. of fencing for a rectangular garden.

    a. What dimensions will give the family the maximum space in their garden? Show your work.

    b. What is the area of a garden of this size? Show your work.

3. It is 45° Fahrenheit. What is the temperature in Celsius? Show your work.

4. A bridge supports weights up to 5 tons. How many kilograms is this?

5. A boat's gas tank holds 190 liters. How many gallons does it hold?

6. Orange juice costs $2.10 for 8 pt. or $1.20 for half a gallon. Which is the better buy?

0-7424-1825-1 *Problem Solving*

Name _____ Date _____

At the Movies

Double bar graphs are used to compare more than one set of data.

Type of Movie	4th Graders	5th Graders
Comedy	25	15
Drama	15	10
Action	25	25
Horror	10	30

1. Complete the graph. Include a scale.

Number of Students

▨ **4th Graders**

■ **5th Graders**

Comedy   Drama   Action   Horror

Type of Movie

2. Which movie type did fourth-grade students prefer? _____

fifth-grade students? _____

3. How were fourth- and fifth-grade preferences similar? How were they different?

COMPARING

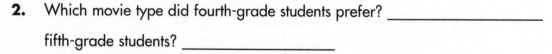

Write a paragraph comparing the data between fourth-grade students and fifth-grade students. Be specific.

92

0-7424-1825-1 *Problem Solving*

Name _____ Date _____

Favorite Sport

Do boys and girls have the same sport preferences? Find out by asking this question:

Which sport do you prefer to play?

1. **Create a survey and tally table.** Brainstorm a list of all the types of sports. If the list is too large, group some of the sports into an "other" category. Make a table. List all the sport categories in the first column. The second column should say "Number of Boys" and the third column should say "Number of Girls."

2. With your teacher's help, **find the best way to conduct the survey** (pass out surveys to classes, ask students during recess, ask other teachers to ask their students, etc.). Survey an equal number of girls and boys.

3. **Conduct the survey.** Ask fifth-grade students the following question: *Which sport do you prefer to play*? Put a tally mark in the table each time someone chooses a sport. Be sure to put the mark in the correct column, depending on if a boy or girl was asked. Once your survey is complete, count the total number of girls and boys in each sport category.

4. **Make a double bar graph.** Use graph paper. List the sport categories across the bottom of the graph. Leave room for two bars above each sport. Label the side of the graph "Number of Students" and make a scale. Make a key that shows which bar is for girls and which is for boys.

5. **Analyze the data.** Describe the similarities and differences between boys' and girls' sports preferences.

ORGANIZING

Describe other ways you could organize and display your data.

0-7424-1825-1 *Problem Solving*

Name _____ Date _____

How Do You Get to School?

Materials: protractor

Transportation	Percentage
Walk	25
Car	20
Bus	45
Bike	10

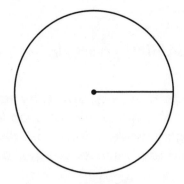

Fifth-grade students were asked how they get to school. The survey results are in the chart.

1. To make an accurate **pie chart,** follow these steps. There are 360 degrees in a circle.

    a. For each transportation percentage, find the corresponding angle measurement. You may want to use a calculator.

        Walk   25% of 360° = _____

        Car   20% of 360° = _____

        Bus   45% of 360° = _____

        Bike   10% of 360° = _____

    b. Place the middle of your protractor onto the center of the circle. Measure the correct angle for each transportation type. Label each section with the correct type of transportation.

2. How does finding the angle measurements help you create an accurate graph?

EXPLAINING

Explain how to find a percentage of a number.

0-7424-1825-1 *Problem Solving*

Name _____ Date _____

Favorite Season

What is your favorite season?

1. **Make a tally table.** Make a 3-column table. Write the seasons, spring, summer, fall, and winter, in the first column. At the top of the second column, write "Number of Students." At the top of the third column, write "Percentage of Students."

2. With your teacher's help, **find the best way to conduct the survey** (pass out surveys to classes, ask students during recess, ask other teachers to ask their students, etc.).

3. **Conduct the survey.** Ask students to choose their favorite season. Put a tally mark next to each student's favorite season. When your survey is complete, count the total number of students in each category. Then find the percentage of students that chose each category.

4. **Make a pie chart.** Use a compass to make a perfect circle. For each season, use the percentages to find the angle measurement for each corresponding section of the circle. Label the section with the name of the season.

5. **Analyze the data.** Describe your results. Is any one season preferred over the others? Are any seasons tied? Which season is liked the least?

REFLECTING

What should the total percentage of all categories be? Why? Should all the sections of the circle be labeled? Why or why not?

0-7424-1825-1 *Problem Solving*

Name _____ Date _____

Everyone's a Critic

Movie critics from across the country were invited to a private showing of 4 new movies. The critics rated the movies on a scale from 0 to 5. The data was put into the histograms below.

The Rise of the Zombies

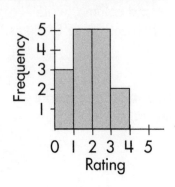

Slapstick Joe

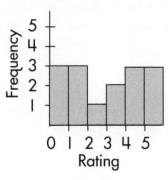

A Day to Remember

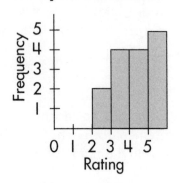

Ralph's Revenge

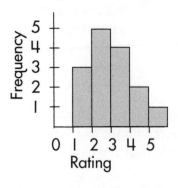

1. Which movie received the worst reviews? Explain your answer.

3. Which movie did the critics disagree about the most? Explain your answer.

2. Which movie has the best chance of being nominated for an Academy Award? Explain your answer.

4. How many critics went to the private showing?

DESCRIBING

Describe each histogram. Be specific.

0-7424-1825-1 *Problem Solving*

Name _____ Date _____

In the News

Headline 1: Land Values Soaring—Centered Around $95,000

Headline 2: Land Values Good—Centered Around $70,000

Headline 3: Land Values Horrible—Centered Around $40,000

All 3 newspaper headlines were based on the following survey data.

Land Values:	$30,000	$40,000	$40,000	$40,000	$40,000
	$40,000	$40,000	$100,000	$100,000	$100,000
	$120,000	$120,000	$200,000	$320,000	

1. Use the terms **mean, median,** and **mode** to explain how each headline is true.

2. Four pieces of property, each valued at $140,000 are added to the survey. How would this change the headlines?

EXPANDING

Give at least 6 data values that fit the following situation: mean = 100, median = 80, mode = none, and range = 160. Explain how you found your answer.

97

Name _____ Date _____

Test Scores

> **Quartiles** group data into quarters (four equal parts).

Nineteen students had the following test results.

67, 75, 45, 89, 91, 70, 80, 85, 77, 62,
72, 95, 81, 76, 55, 59, 68, 88, 100

I. Arrange the test scores from least to greatest.

2. Find and circle the **median** of the scores. Median = _____

3. Find and put an **x** on the median of the lower half of the scores. This is called the **first quartile.**

Q1 = _____

4. Find and put an **x** on the median of the upper half of the scores. This is called the **third quartile.**

Q3 = _____

5. If your score is 85, is it in the upper quartile (greater than the third quartile)?

EXPANDING

What percentage of the data is below the first quartile? Below the median? Below the third quartile? What percentage of the data is between the first and third quartile? How does knowing this help you compare a score with those of the rest of the class?

0-7424-1825-1 *Problem Solving*

Name _____ Date _____

Standing in Line

Materials: 4 cubes of different colors

> **Number of Possible Combinations**
>
> = # of 1st options x   # of 2nd options x # of 3rd options . . .

1. Dashon, Jaleesa, and Todd are standing in line. How many different ways do you think they can stand in a line?

Write your prediction. _____

2. Use the formula at the top of the page. There are three places to stand in line: first, second, or third.

    a. How many people could be in the front of the line? Write your answer above the word *first*.

    b. If one child is standing in the first spot, how many children are left to stand in the second spot? Write your answer above the word *second*.

    c. If the first and second spots are taken, how many children are left to stand the third spot? Write your answer above the word *third*.

    d. Use the formula to calculate the answer.

Number of ways to stand in line =

_____ x _____ x _____ = _____
  (first)   (second)   (third)

0-7424-1825-1 *Problem Solving*

Name _____ Date _____

Standing in Line (cont.)

3. Choose a colored cube to represent each child. Put three cubes in order. Record the colors. Then put the cubes in a different order. Repeat until you have found each possible combination.

   a. Make a list of all the possible ways the three children could stand in line.

   b. How many different cube combinations did you find? _____

   c. Does this match the answer you found using the formula? _____

4. Lynn, Kaitlin, Adam, and Maria sit down at the table to eat. There are four different places at the table: the head, foot, left side, and right side. How many different ways can the four of them sit at the table?

   a. Use cubes or make a list to find the answer. Record your work on another sheet of paper.

   b. Use the formula to find the answer.

   $$\underset{\text{(head)}}{\text{_____}} \times \underset{\text{(left side)}}{\text{_____}} \times \underset{\text{(right side)}}{\text{_____}} \times \underset{\text{(foot)}}{\text{_____}} = \text{_____}$$

COMPARING

Which solution method do you prefer, the formula or the cubes? Why?

0-7424-1825-1 *Problem Solving*

Name _____ Date _____

Keep on Rolling

Materials: a pair of dice

Diana and Kida are playing a game. They both roll a die and then add the 2 numbers together. Diana gets a point if the sum is less than 7. Kida gets a point if the sum is greater than 7. Neither gets a point if the sum is 7. Who is most likely to win the game?

1. Make a prediction.

2. Test your guess. Roll 2 dice 36 times and record the sums on a separate piece of paper. Which was rolled more, a sum greater than 7 or less than 7?

3. Make a chart to show the possible sums.

Diana's Die

+	1	2	3	4	5	6
1	2	3				
2						
3				7		
4						
5						
6						

(row labels on left: **Kida's Die**)

4. Use your chart. What sum are you most likely to get when you roll 2 dice? What sums are you least likely to get?

5. Who is most likely to win the game?

EXPANDING

If you roll 2 regular dice, what is the chance you will get doubles? Explain.

0-7424-1825-1 *Problem Solving*

Name _____ Date _____

Random Draw

Materials: brown paper bag, colored cubes (may be simulated with colored cardboard squares)

The 3 bags below each hold 10 cubes. The cubes may be blue, red, yellow, or green. Read the clues below each bag. Then color the cubes to match the clue.

Bag 1:
Blue, yellow, and green are equally likely to be drawn. Red is least likely to be drawn.

Bag 2:
Yellow and green are equally likely to be drawn but are less likely than either blue or red. Blue is more likely to be drawn than red.

Bag 3:
Yellow is least likely to be drawn. Blue is most likely to be drawn. Red has a better chance to be drawn than green.

Test your answers. Choose one of the bags. Put the combination of cubes you have chosen in the bag. Draw one cube out, record the color, replace the cube, and shake the bag. Repeat this 20 times. Use tally marks to record your results.

Color	Tally Marks
blue	
red	
green	
yellow	

REFLECTING

Did your results match the clue? Do you think you need to change the color combination? Why or why not?

0-7424-1825-1 *Problem Solving*

Name _____ Date _____

Spin Out

Jacob and Antwon are playing a game with a spinner. Each spins the spinner. Then they add the 2 numbers together. If the sum is even, Jacob gets a point. If the sum is odd, Antwon gets a point. Who has the better chance of winning?

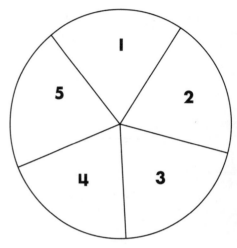

1. Make a prediction. _____

2. Test your guess. Make a spinner like the one above. Choose a partner and play the game. Record the results on another piece of paper. The game ends after 20 spins each.

3. Which player won, even or odd? _____

4. Make a table of possible spinner combinations. Circle all the even numbers.

	1	2	3	4	5
1					
2					
3					
4					
5					

5. Are there more even or odd sums? _____

EXTENDING

What would happen if you multiplied the 2 numbers instead of adding them? Who would most likely win, the person with odd numbers or the person with even numbers? Explain how you know.

0-7424-1825-1 *Problem Solving*

Name _____   Date _____

Create Your Own Problems

1. Choose a question and design a survey. Compare boys' and girls' answers to the question. Make an appropriate graph to display the data. Write a summary of your results.

Possible survey questions: *Which type of book do you like to read?*

What type of television shows do you prefer?

What is your favorite holiday?

What is your favorite school subject?

2. Make up a set of 19 test scores. Find the quartiles. Ask at least 3 questions about the data (If you scored a ____, would you be above/below the _____?). Ask a partner to answer the questions.

3. Choose 10 cubes of different colors. Write a clue that describes the chance of getting those colors. Give your clue to a partner. Have your partner choose cubes to match the clue. Does the cube combination match yours? If not, does it match the clues? Do you need to change the clue so there is only 1 possible answer?

4. Make up 2 games involving rolling 2 dice and finding the sum. Assign points based on the sum. Slant the game so that one sum has a greater chance of being rolled than the other. Explain the rules of the game to a partner and let your partner choose his or her sum. See if your partner will choose the "winning" sum.

0-7424-1825-1 *Problem Solving*

Name _____ Date _____

Check Your Skills

Answer these questions on another piece of paper.

1. A survey was taken of fifth-grade students. The survey asked students to choose their favorite school subject: math, English, science, or social studies. Every student chose a favorite subject. The count for each subject was recorded as a percentage.

    a. What type of graph would most likely be used to display the data? Why?

    b. Make a graph showing the results you think would occur. List the exact percentages you used to make your graph.

2. Here are 19 test scores.

    67, 75, 63, 89, 91, 70, 80, 85, 77, 62, 72, 95, 73, 77, 55, 59, 54, 98, 100

    a. Find the mean, median, and mode test score.

    b. Find the first and third quartiles.

3. Five people, Jeremy, Jenny, Joel, Jill, and Jana, are standing in line for concert tickets. While waiting, they often switch places. How many different ways could they stand in line? Explain how you found your answer.

4. There are 10 cubes in a bag. There is an equal chance of drawing a yellow or green cube, but blue is more likely to be drawn than either. Red is most likely to be drawn. How many cubes of each color cube are in the bag?

0-7424-1825-1 *Problem Solving*

Cumulative Post Test

Answer the following questions on a separate piece of paper.

1. Which of the following numbers are prime? How do you know?

    31, 39, 42, 69, 73, 77, 83

2. What is another way to calculate 7 x 12, using multiplication and addition? Draw a model that shows both expressions are the same.

3. There are 120 students in the fifth grade at Pleasantville Elementary. On Fridays, $\frac{1}{5}$ of the students are taking Band, $\frac{1}{4}$ are taking Gym, 30% are in their classrooms, and the remainder are taking Art. How many students are taking each subject? Show your work.

4. Ms. Denson collected $990 from her students for a class trip. The cost of the trip was $45 per student. How many students are going on the trip?

5. Complete the pattern. Describe the pattern.

    4, 12, 36, _____, _____, _____

6. Chu, Mara, Lourdes, and Alys were the top 4 finishers of the 100-meter sprint. Chu did not place second. Alys placed better than Chu. Lourdes finished after 2 others. Only one person placed between Mara and Lourdes. In what order did the girls place?

7. Find the numbers that make all 3 equations true.

    ▰ + ▰ + ▰ = 27

    ▰ – ▲ = 4

    ▲ x 2 = ⬡

     0-7424-1825-1 *Problem Solving*

Cumulative Post Test (cont.)

8. Concert tickets cost $25 each. Melony buys them from Tickets R Us, which charges a flat fee of $2 to process tickets. Let **T** be the number of tickets. Let **P** be the price Melony pays. Write an equation. **P** = _____

9. A nonagon has 9 sides. Find the sum of all the angles in a nonagon. Show your work.

10. A regular nonagon has angles that measure 140°. Can a tiling pattern be created using only nonagons? Explain.

11. A rectangular garden has a perimeter of 36 ft. What dimensions will provide the most space in the garden? Explain.

12. It is 12° Celsius. What is the temperature in Fahrenheit? Show your work.

13. Laundry detergent comes in 2 sizes: 24 oz. for $2.56 or 36 oz. for $3.42. Which is the better buy?

14. A survey was taken of fourth- and fifth-grade students. Students were asked to choose their favorite type of ice cream: vanilla, strawberry, chocolate, or other. What type of graph would be best to compare fourth- and fifth-grade choices?

15. How many different ways could teams place in the Final Four playoffs? Explain.

0-7424-1825-1 *Problem Solving*

Pattern Block Templates

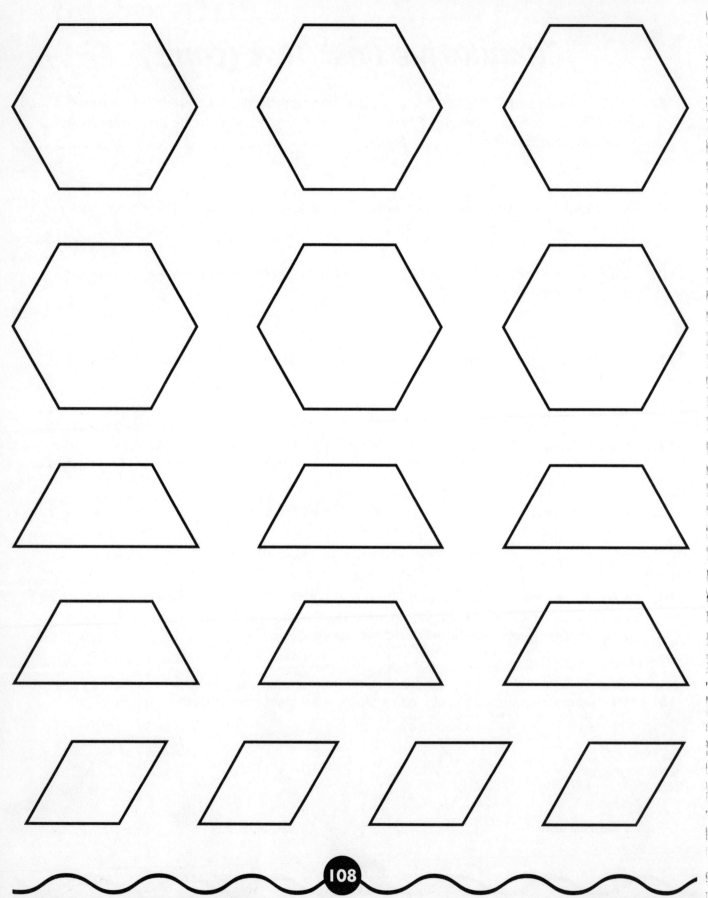

0-7424-1825-1 *Problem Solving*

Pattern Block Templates

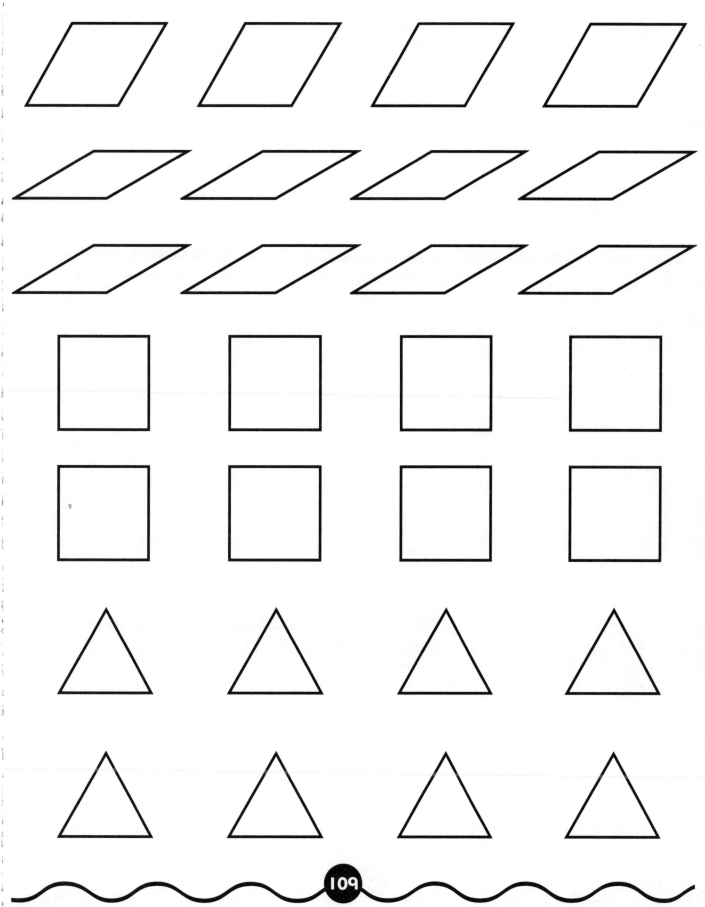

0-7424-1825-1 *Problem Solving*

Dollar Bill Templates

0-7424-1825-1 *Problem Solving*

Answer Key

Problem-Solving Challenge **7–8**

1. $\frac{2}{6} = 0.33 = 33\%$, $\frac{4}{6} = 0.668 = 66.8\%$, $\frac{5}{6} = .835 = 83.5\%$

2. 15 boxes of 18   3. 5 x 8; check models

4. $41.34   5. 625

6. OUT: 16, 24, 48, 72, 88; Rule: IN x 8

7. **a.** 12 **b.** 882 **c.** 7

8. $C = 25 \times H$. The area of the base is 25 square inches, so 25 cubes will fit along the bottom of the box. There will be **H** layers of cubes in the box. So, there will be 25 x **H** cubes in the box. **C** measures the volume of the box.

9. A parallelogram is a quadrilateral where the opposite sides are parallel and congruent.

10. Find the sum of the angles that will go around a point. If the sum is exactly 360°, the shapes will create a tiling pattern.

11. 96 cards. 5 ft. is 60 in. (12 x 5) and 2 ft. is 24 in. (12 x 2). The desk has a surface area of 1,440 square inches (60 x 24). Each index card has an area of 15 square inches (3 x 5). 1,440 ÷ 15 = 96.

12. 12.5 cm (5 x 2.5)   13. 136.8 L (36 x 3.8)

14. 7.15 T. (6,500 kg x 2.2 lb./kg = 14,300 lb.; 14,300lb. ÷ 2,000 lb./T. = 7.15 T.)

15. median = 77, first quartile = 65, third quartile = 90; 25% of the students scored 65 or lower, 50% scored 77 or lower, and 75% scored 90 or lower.

16. 4 green, 3 red, 2 blue, 2 orange, and 1 yellow

A Slice of the Pie **9**

1. $\frac{1}{2} = 0.5$; $\frac{1}{3} = 0.33$; $\frac{1}{4} = 0.25$; $\frac{1}{5} = 0.2$; $\frac{1}{6} = 0.16$; $\frac{1}{7} = 0.14$; $\frac{1}{8} = 0.125$; $\frac{1}{9} = 0.11$; $\frac{1}{10} = 0.1$

2.

Reflecting As the denominator gets larger, the fraction gets smaller at a decreasing rate. The distance between consecutive fractions gets smaller as the denominator increases by 1. The denominator of the fraction represents the number of pieces the whole is broken into. The more pieces cut, the smaller each piece must be.

Freaky Fractions **10**

1. $\frac{2}{3} = \frac{1}{3} + \frac{1}{3} \approx 0.33 + 0.33 \approx 0.66$

2. $\frac{2}{5} = \frac{1}{5} + \frac{1}{5} = 0.2 + 0.2 = 0.4$
$\frac{3}{5} = \frac{2}{5} + \frac{1}{5} = 0.4 + 0.2 = 0.6$
$\frac{4}{5} = \frac{3}{5} + \frac{1}{5} = 0.6 + 0.2 = 0.8$

3. $\frac{2}{6} = \frac{1}{6} + \frac{1}{6} \approx 0.17 + 0.17 \approx 0.34$;
$\frac{3}{6} = \frac{2}{6} + \frac{1}{6} \approx 0.34 + 0.17 \approx 0.51$;

$\frac{4}{6} = \frac{3}{6} + \frac{1}{6} \approx 0.51 + 0.17 \approx 0.68$;
$\frac{5}{6} = \frac{4}{6} + \frac{1}{6} \approx 0.68 + 0.17 \approx 0.85$

4. **a.** $\frac{2}{3} > \frac{3}{5}$ **b.** $\frac{1}{5} > \frac{1}{3}$ **c.** $\frac{3}{4} < \frac{4}{5}$ **d.** $\frac{3}{5} > \frac{1}{2}$

Explaining Answers may vary. Students could compare the decimal equivalencies found in problems 1–3, find common denominators, or draw pictures.

Even or Odd? **11**

1. Answers will vary.

2. Answers will vary. Each person or group could test different pairs to create a larger class sample.

3. Make sure students do not use their test cases as proof that the hypothesis is true. Multiple test cases *support* the hypothesis that the product of 2 even numbers is even, but they do not *prove* it to be true. Encourage students to use reasoning to show why it will be true in all cases. The product of any two numbers will be the same as the product of their prime factors. Two is a factor of every even number. If you multiply the even number by any other number, the resulting number will also have 2 as a factor, which makes it even.

4. *The product of an even number and an odd number is even.* See the answer to problem 3 for the reasoning. *The product of 2 odd numbers is odd.* The product of any two numbers will be the same as the product of their prime factors. Since neither odd number can have a factor of 2, their product also cannot have a factor of 2.

Reflecting It takes only one example that doesn't fit the hypothesis to disprove it. To prove a hypothesis, you must either test every single possibility or use logical reasoning and known facts.

Finding Factors **12**

1. **a.** the last digit is even **b.** the last digit is 5 or 0 **c.** the last digit is 0

2. A number has a factor of 3 if the sum of its digits is a multiple of 3.

3. A number has a factor of 9 if the sum of its digits is a multiple of 9.

4. 4 is a factor of: 128; 2,464; 272; 388; 2,300; 4,512. Yes, the trick always works (if you think of any number ending in 00 as being "100," which is divisible by 4).

Expanding 6: *A number has a factor of 6 if it has 2 AND 3 as factors (an even number whose digits have a sum that is a multiple of 3).* 7: *There is no "trick" for 7.* 8: *Any number that has a factor of 8 will also have a factor of 4.* This helps eliminate many possibilities. If a number does not have a factor of 4, then it also won't have a factor of 8. If a number does have a factor of 4, then it must be tested to see if 8 is also a factor.

0-7424-1825-1 *Problem Solving*

Answer Key

Positively Prime **13**

1. 2 is the only even prime number. All other even numbers have a factor of 2.
2. Every prime number, except 2, is odd. But, not all odd numbers are prime. 9 is odd and has a factor of 3.
3. No. The product will automatically have 2 additional factors besides itself and 1.
4. The multiplication table shows many numbers that are **not** prime. If a number is found on the table (so long as it is not in the "1 x" row or column), then it is not prime.
5. **a–e.** no
   f. Answers may vary. **g.** $143 \div 11 = 13$ **h.** No.
6. 2, 3, 5, 7, 11, 13, 17, 19, 23, 29, 31, 37, 41, 43, 47, 53, 59, 61, 67, 71, 73, 79, 83, 89, and 97

Explaining Answers may vary. Students could use a 100 chart and cross out all multiples of the numbers 2–10. They could then test the remaining numbers to see if any have prime factors.

Which Is More? **14**

1. **a.** 12 boxes of 24 **b.** $15 \times 18 = 270$; $12 \times 24 = 288$
2. **a.** 16 bags of 25 **b.** $12 \times 30 = 360$; $16 \times 25 = 400$
3. **a.** 12 ft. by 14 ft. **b.** $12 \times 14 = 168$; $15 \times 11 = 165$

Reflecting Multiplication was used to find the answers.

Distance, Rate, and Time **15**

1. **a.** 27 miles away **b.** multiplication
2. **a.** $27 \div 9 = 3$ hours **b.** yes **c.** Time = Distance ÷ Rate

Reflecting The equations use opposite operations. They are inverses.

Multiplication Madness **16**

1. **a.** $8 \times 4 = 32$ **b.** $4 \times 8 = 32$
2. **a.** 15 **b.** $5 \times 3 = 15$ **c.** Students should draw 5 circles in each of the 3 boxes. **d.** $3 \times 5 = 15$

Reflecting In each problem, the order of the numbers being multiplied was changed. This did not change the answers.

Multiplication Madness **17**

1. **a.** $7 \times 11 = 77$ **b.** $7 \times 8 + 7 \times 3 = 77$ **c.** The answers are the same.
2. **a.** $5 \times 13 = 65$. Students should draw an area model with 5 rows and 13 columns. **b.** Answers will vary. One possible answer is $5 \times 10 + 5 \times 3$ **c.** The answers are the same.

Expanding Answers will vary. One possible answer is $6 \times 12 + 6 \times 2$.

Supermarket Dilemma **18**

1. Answers may vary depending on what students believe is the shortest possible time for each conversation. If each conversation takes 1 minute, he would have called 180 customers.
2. He could possibly have spent 3 hours on the phone with 1 person.
3. 180 minutes ÷ 20 minutes per person = 9 people

4. 180 minutes ÷ 3 minutes per person = 60 people
5. 180 minutes ÷ 45 people = 4 minutes per person

Expanding Answers will vary.

Candy Bar Calculations **19**

1. $50 \times 50 \times 100 = 250,000$
2. $1,000 \div 54 = 18.5$. 19 boxes will need to ship the candy bars. One of the boxes will not be full.
3. 1 carton and 8 boxes will be needed. The last box will not be full. There are 2,592 (48 x 54) candy bars in each carton. 408 (3,000 – 2,592) candy bars will be left over. 408 candy bars ÷ 54 bars per box = 7.5 boxes.
4. 2,721,600 candy bars will be stored in 10 warehouses (2,592 x 105 x 10).

Explaining Answers may vary.

Pleasantville Elementary **20**

1. **a.** Students should circle 6 sets of 5 squares.
   b. 5 students in each set; $\frac{1}{6}$ **c.** 5 sets of 5 is 25 students
2. **a.** $\frac{2}{5}$ is less than half, so there are more boys in the class.
   b. Five equal sets should be circled. There are 6 students in each set. **c.** $\frac{2}{5}$ means 2 sets out of 5 are girls. 2 sets of 6 students = 12 girls.

Reflecting Answers may vary.

Pleading the Fifth **21**

1. **a.** $\frac{1}{5}$ **b.** Students should have $\frac{2}{10}$ shaded.
   c. $\frac{2}{10} = \frac{20}{100}$. **d.** 20%
2. $\frac{2}{5} = \frac{1}{5} + \frac{1}{5} = 20\% + 20\% = 40\%$
3. $\frac{3}{5} = 60\%$; $\frac{4}{5} = 80\%$

Expanding $\frac{2}{3} \approx 33\% + 33\% \approx 66\%$

How Many? **22**

1. **a.** 20 **b.** 25%   2. **a.** 32 **b.** $\frac{2}{5}$
3. **a.** 35% **b.** $\frac{7}{20}$ **c.** 28

Explaining Answers may vary.

How Many? **23**

1. $\frac{1}{3} \times 300 = 100$ 2. $\frac{1}{4} \times 300 = 75$
3. $\frac{2}{5} \times 300 = 120$
4. **a.** $300 - (100 + 75 + 120) = 5$ **b.** $\frac{5}{300} = \frac{1}{60}$

Expanding 33% ride the bus, 25% ride in a car, 40% walk, and 2% ride bikes. The sum of the percentages is 100%. This makes sense if these are all the possible ways the students get to school.

0-7424-1825-1 *Problem Solving*

Answer Key

Parking Problems 24
1. 600 cars is the maximum $(2,400 \div 4 = 600)$
2. 100 motorcycles $(\frac{1}{12} \times 2,400 = 200$ wheels; 200 wheels $\div$ 2 wheels per motorcycle = 100 motorcycles)
3. 72 tires on tractor trailers $(4 \times 18 = 72$ tires)
4. 532 four-wheel vehicles $(2,400 - 200 - 72 = 2,128$ tires; 2,128 tires $\div$ 4 tires per vehicle = 532 vehicles)

Explaining Make sure answer to #2 is $\frac{1}{12}$ of the tires $(\frac{200}{2,400} = \frac{1}{12})$. The total number of wheels should add up to 2,400 $(100 \times 2 + 72 + 532 \times 4 = 2,400)$.

Pizza! Pizza! Pizza! 25
1. There are a total of 36 slices $(12 + 9 + 15)$. Each person gets 4 slices $(36 \div 9 = 4)$.
2. Each person could have 3 slices. There would be 6 slices left over $(36 \div 10 = 3 \text{ R}6)$.
3. $\frac{1}{9} (\frac{4}{36})$ 4. 12 slices $(\frac{1}{3} \times 36)$
5. 20 slices $(\frac{1}{3} + \frac{1}{9} = \frac{3}{9} + \frac{1}{9} = \frac{4}{9}$ eaten; $\frac{5}{9}$ left; $\frac{5}{9} \times 36 = 20$ slices left)
6. Yes. Each person gets 5 slices $(20 \div 4 = 5)$.

Reflecting Answers will vary.

Nature Camp 26
1. 56 students $(\$4,200 \div \$75)$
2. a. No. There are 32 boys and only 20 bunks $(\frac{4}{7} \times 56 = 32)$.
   b. 24 bunks $(56 - 32 = 24, \text{ or } \frac{3}{7} \times 56 = 24)$
   c.
   56 students: 7 sets of 8
   ▪ 4 out of 7 sets are boys: $4 \times 8 = 32$
   ☐ 3 out of 7 sets are girls: $3 \times 8 = 24$
   $24 + 32 = 56$

Describing Multiply the fraction by the number.

Nature Camp 27
1. a. 12 adults $(0.15 \times 80 = 12)$
   b. 68 campers $(80 - 12 = 68, \text{ or } 85\% \text{ of } 80 = 68)$
2. a. 720 meals (3 meals per day x 3 days x 80 people)
   b. 40 dozen eggs (2 eggs per person x 80 people x 3 days = 480 eggs; $480 \div 12 = 40$ dozen)

Reflecting Multiplication can be used in each problem.

Toys, Toys, Toys 28
1. a. 300 toys for children under 3 $(\frac{1}{4} \times 1,200 = 300)$
   b. 360 toys for children ages 3–8 $(0.30 \times 1,200 = 360)$
   c. 480 toys for children ages 9–12 $(\frac{2}{5} \times 1,200 = 480)$

   d. 5% are for kids over age 12 $(\frac{1}{4} = 25\%$ and $\frac{2}{5} = 40\%$; $100\% - 25\% - 30\% - 40\% = 5\%)$
2. a. 7 wagons $(\frac{1}{3} \times 84 = 28$ wheels; 28 wheels $\div$ 4 wheels per wagon = 7 wagons)
   b. 18 tricycles $(\frac{9}{14} \times 84 = 54$ wheels; 54 wheels $\div$ 3 wheels per tricycle = 18 tricycles)
   c. 1 scooter $(84 - 28 - 54 = 2$ wheels left)

Reflecting Both show what portion of the amount. To find the portion, you multiply the fraction or percentage by the number.

Is It Enough? 29
1. 80%   2. $0.80 \times 112 = \$89.60$
3. $78.40 (30% off = 70% of the regular price; $0.70 \times 112 = 78.4$)
4. $0.04 \times 78.4 = \$3.14$
5. Yes. $78.40 + $3.14 = $81.54. She has $85.

Explaining If it is 25% off, that means the sale price is 75% of the regular price. Multiply 0.75 by the regular price.

Planning a Picnic 30–31
1. a. $0.25 \times 25,400 = 6,350$ more hamburgers; $6,350 + 25,400 = 31,750$ hamburgers
   b. $1.25 \times 25,400 = 31,750$ hamburgers
   c. Answers may vary.
2. 37,800 hot dogs   3. 70,000 ice-cream bars
4. 28,800 pounds of French fries
5. 52,806 soda cans

Explaining 1,101 cases will need to be ordered $(52,806 \div 48 = 1,100.125)$.

Check Your Skills 33
1. a. Store 1 had the better deal, 70% of its original price.
   b. She saved $22.50 $(0.70 \times \$75 = \$52.50;$ $75 - $52.50 = $22.50)$
2. a. 414 passengers on jet 2 $(0.9 \times 460 = 414)$
   b. 400 passengers on jet 4 $(\frac{5}{6} \times 480 = 400)$
   c. 1,754 passengers $(460 + 414 + 480 + 400)$
3. $7 \times 16 = 112$ a. $16 \times 7 = 112$ b. Answers may vary. One possible solution is $7 \times 10 + 7 \times 6 = 112$.

Shape Patterns 34
1. The shapes rotate counter clockwise around the corners.
2. a. The numbers increase by 2 each time.
   b. The numbers increase by 2 each time.
   c. The bottom number is 3 more than the top number.
   d. The shading rotates clockwise around the corners.
   e.

Expanding Answers will vary.

113

Answer Key

Function Machine 35
 1. 40, 45; Rule: OUT = IN x 5
 2. 9, 10, 11; Rule: OUT = IN ÷ 5
 Describing The rules are inverses of one another. They both use the number 5, but one is multiplication and the other is division.

Do the Two-Step 36
1.

IN	2	3	4	5	6	7	9
OUT	5	6	7	8	9	10	12
IN	6	6	7	8	9	10	12
OUT	10	12	14	16	18	20	24

Rule 1: OUT = IN + 3   Rule 2: OUT = IN x 2

2.

IN	3	4	5	6	7	9	10
OUT	9	12	15	18	21	27	30
IN	9	12	15	18	21	27	20
OUT	6	9	12	15	18	24	27

Rule 1: OUT = IN x 3   Rule 2: OUT = IN – 3
Explaining Use the first rule to change the number. Then, use the OUT value as the IN value of the second rule.

Number Patterns 37
 1. a. growing pattern **b.** no **c.** All the columns have the rule x 2.
 2. a. growing pattern **b.** no **c.** Add the previous two numbers to get the next number.
 3. C6: 29, 58, 116, 232
 Expanding Answers will vary.

More Number Patterns 38
 1. For each row, add the number that is shown in the first column each time.
 2. a. decreasing pattern **b.** no
   c. C1: Subtract by consecutive integers each time, starting with 2 (–2, –3, –4…)
   C2: Subtract by even consecutive integers each time, starting with 4 (–4, –6, –8…)
   C3: Subtract by integers that go up by 3 each time, starting with 6 (–6, –9, –12…)
   C4: Subtract by integers that go up by 4 each time, starting with 8 (–8, –12, –16…)
   C5: Subtract by integers that go up by 5 each time, starting with 10 (–10, –15, –20…)
   C6: Subtract by integers that go up by 6 each time, starting with 12 (–12, –18, –24…)
   d. The starting amount of decrease goes up by twos. The amount of change between each number goes up by one

from one column to the next.
 e. 120, 108, 90, 66, 36
 Explaining Answers may vary.

Who's Taller? 39
 1. a. Rashawn, Danielle, Tamequa, Joaquín
   b. Answers may vary. Tamequa must be third in height, since she is taller than exactly 2 of the children. Since Danielle is taller than Rashawn but not Joaquín, Rawshawn must be shortest, Danielle must be the next shortest, and Joaquín must be the tallest.
 2. a. Since Joaquín is neither the shortest nor the tallest, put x's below 1 and 4 next to his name. Since Rashawn and Danielle are both shorter than 2 children, neither can be the tallest or the 2nd tallest. Put an x below the 3 and 4 next to Rashawn and Danielle. This means Tamequa must be the tallest. Put a circle below the 4 next to Tamequa. Since Tamequa is the tallest, she can not be in any of the other places, so put x's below 1, 2, and 3 next to Tamequa. This means Joaquín must be third. Since Rashawn is shorter than Danielle, Rashawn is the shortest, and Danielle comes next.
   b. Rashawn, Danielle, Joaquín, Tamequa
 Organizing Answers may vary.

All About Order 40
 Height: Rashawn, Joaquín, Danielle, Tamequa
 Age: Joaquín, Tamequa, Danielle, Rashawn
 • Since Danielle is not the shortest, put an x below the 1 next to her name in the height chart.
 • Rashawn is older than at least 2 children, so he is not the youngest or the second youngest. Put x's below the 1 and 2 next to his name in the age chart.
 • Danielle is not the shortest child, and the shortest child is the oldest. So, Danielle cannot be the oldest. Put an x below the 4 next to her name in the age chart.
 • Since Joaquín is taller than one other child, he is ranked second in height. Put a circle below the 2 next to his name in the height chart. Put x's in the remaining grid squares in Joaquín's row and the 2 column.
 • Danielle is the only child to have the same ranking in both height and age. The height chart shows that Danielle is not ranked first or second in height. This means she is also not ranked first or second in age. Put x's below the 1 and 2 next to her name in the age chart. Danielle must be third in age, which also makes her third in height. Put circles below the 3's in both charts. Put x's in the remaining grid squares in Danielle's row and the 3 column of both charts.
 • According to the age chart, the only remaining opening for Rashawn is below the 4. This means Rashawn is the oldest. Put a circle below the 4 next to his name and put x's in the remaining spaces in the 4 column of the age chart.

114

    0-7424-1825-1 *Problem Solving*

Answer Key

- *Only* Danielle has the same ranking in both height and age. Since Rashawn is the oldest, he is not the tallest. Put an x below the 4 next to his name in the height chart. There is only one remaining opening for Rashawn's height, which is below the 1. Rashawn is the shortest. Put a circle below the 1 and put x's in the remaining grid squares in column 1. The height chart now shows that Tamequa must be the tallest.
- The age chart shows that either Tamequa or Joaquín must be the youngest. Since Joaquín is ranked second in height, he is not second in age. Joaquín is the youngest, and Tamequa is ranked second in age.

Reflecting Danielle is not the oldest.

Missing Numbers 41
1. **a.** 1, 16; 2, 8; 16, 1; 8, 2
   b. Answers may vary.
   c. factors of 16
2. There are multiple answers. Some possible answers are 12, 2; 18, 3; 24, 4; 30, 5

Reflecting No. There are an infinite number of solutions.

Missing Numbers 42
1. $9 + 9 + 9 = 27$ 2. $13 + 13 = 26$ 3. No.
4. Answers may vary. Example: $8 - 8 = 0$
5. Answers may vary. Example: $9 \div 9 = 1$

Expanding No matter what values you use for the star, the heart will always be 0. No matter what values you use for the smiley face, the flower will always be 1.

Missing Numbers 43
1. 5   2. 100   3. 4   4. 90   5. 12
6. triangle = 5, hexagon = 6, trapezoid = 4

Explaining Answers may vary.

Finding Unknowns 44
Room 9: **B** = 12, **A** = 10, **S** = 5
Room 10: **B** = 10, **A** = 15, **S** = 5
Room 11: **B** = 8, **A** = 16, **S** = 4; 28 votes in all

Explaining Answers may vary.

Making Equations 45
1. **a.** 36 **b.** 8 **c.** 36 x 8 = 288 **d.** volume
2. 36 x 5 = 180 cubes   3. 36 x 10 = 360 cubes
4. **C** = 36 x **H**

Expanding **C** = 16 x **H**

Making Equations 46
1. **a.** $4 x 3 = $12 **b.** $4 x 4 = $16 **c.** M = $4 x **H**
2. **a.** 5 x $5 = $25 **b.** $25 + $8 = $33 **c.** 7 x $5 + $8 = $43
   d. **C** = $5 x **T** + $8

Describing **C** = $10 x **L**. Descriptions may vary.

Tall Towers 47–48
1.
Height of Tower (units)	1	2	3	4	5
Surface Area (square units)	10	16	22	28	34

2. 34 square units
3. The surface area increases by 6 square units.
4. 6 x 10 + 4 = 64
5. There are six square units of surface area around the sides of each layer. Since there are 10 layers, that is 60 square units. Plus, there are 2 square units on the top and 2 on the bottom. 60 + 4 = 64.
6. **S** = 6 x **H** + 4

Reflecting Answers may vary.

Show Me the Money! 49–50
1.
Birthday	12	13	14	15	16	17	18
Total Saved	1,000	2,000	3,000	4,000	5,000	6,000	7,000

2. $7,000
3. Sara's fund grows $1,000 each year, which is a steady rate.
4.
Birthday	12	13	14	15	16	17	18
Amt. Rcvd. Each Birthday	100	200	400	800	1,600	3,200	6,400
Total Amt. Saved	100	300	700	1,500	3,100	6,300	12,700

5. $12,700
6. The money grows slowly at first and then more rapidly. It grows at an increasing rate.
7. Sara will have more money for college if she chooses option 2.
8. If the plan ended after her sixteenth birthday, she should choose option 1. She would have $5,000 with option 1 and only $3,100 with option 2.

Comparing Option 1 grows at a steady rate. Option 2 grows at an increasing rate. The amount of time the plan is in effect does make a difference. Sara will have more money saved with option 1 up until her sixteenth birthday. After her seventeenth birthday, option 2 will be slightly higher. After her eighteenth birthday, option 2 gives her a much higher amount.

Growing Patterns 51
1. 4 more tiles are added to each shape.
2. 8, 12, 16, 20, 24   3. 44; 64

Describing The pattern grows at a steady rate, adding 4 tiles per shape.

Check Your Skills 53
1. OUT: 8, 16, 20, 28, 44, 48 Rule: OUT = IN x 4
2. **a.** diamond = 9 **b.** clover = 7
3. Gary, Lisa, Becky, Allyson
4. **a.** $30 **b.** $72 **c.** **C** = $6 x **T**
5. **a.** 35, 57, 92, 149; Rule: add the previous 2 numbers
   b. 300, 60, 12; Rule: ÷ 5
   c. 108, 324, 972, 2,916; Rule: x 3

115

Answer Key

A Class by Itself **54–55**
  1. a. scalene, right **b.** isosceles, obtuse **c.** scalene, acute
    d. equilateral, acute **e.** scalene, obtuse **f.** isosceles, right
    g. isosceles, acute **h.** scalene, acute **i.** scalene, obtuse

2.

	obtuse	acute	right
scalene	e, i	c, h	a
equilateral		d	
isosceles	b	g	f

    a. equilateral obtuse and equilateral right
    b. It is impossible to draw shapes to match these
      characteristics. All equilateral triangles are acute.
    c. All angles of an equilateral triangle are 60°.
Explaining Answers may vary. Both characteristics
are necessary to identify the type of triangle.

Pondering Polygons **56**
  1–4. Answers may vary.
Describing A polygon is a closed shape with straight edges that
do not overlap.

Parallelograms **57**
  1–3. Answers may vary.
  4. Parallelograms are quadrilaterals where the opposite sides are
    congruent and parallel.
Explaining Answers may vary.

Quadrilaterals **58**

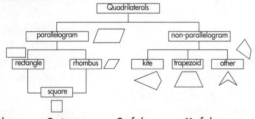

  1. false   **2.** true   **3.** false   **4.** false
  5. true   **6.** false   **7.** false   **8.** true

Angle Sums **59**
  1. pentagon
  2. a. 3 **b.** 180° **c.** The sum of all the angles in the triangles will
    equal the angle sum of the pentagon. **d.** 180 x 3 = 540°
  3. pentagon   **4. a.** 3 **b.** 180 x 3 = 540°.
  5. Both polygons have 5 sides. Any 5-sided polygon can be
    divided into 3 triangles, for an angle sum of 540°
Reflecting All pentagons can be divided into 3 triangles by
drawing diagonals between vertices. All pentagons have an angle
sum of 540°.

Angle Sums **60**

# sides	# triangles	Angle Sum
3	1	180
4	2	360
5	3	540
6	4	720
7	5	900
8	6	1,080
9	7	1,260

  1. The number of triangles will be 2 less than the number of
    sides. $t = n - 2$
  2. The angle sum of a polygon will be the number of triangles
    multiplied by 180°. $S = t \times 180$
Explaining To find the angle sum of any polygon, first draw
diagonals to divide the shape into triangles. There will always be
2 fewer triangles than there are sides of the polygon. Then,
multiply the number of triangles by 180°. $S = (n - 2) \times 180°$.

Prisms and Pyramids **61**
  1. Answers may vary.
  2. Prisms have 2 parallel and congruent polygon bases
    connected by rectangular faces.
    Pyramids have 1 polygon base with triangular faces meeting
    at a vertex (or peak).
Explaining Answers may vary.

Plotting Pleasantville **62–63**
  1.

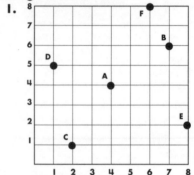

  2. Routes may vary.
  3. a. 6 blocks **b.** 11 blocks **c.** 10 blocks **d.** 5 blocks
  4. a. (7, 6) **b.** (2, 1) **c.** (1, 5) **d.** (8, 2)
Expanding Answers will vary.

Finding Routes **64–65**
  1. a. (8, 9) **b.** (5, 1) **c.** (12, 1) **d.** (9, 3) **e.** (4, 3) **f.** (6, 6)
    g. (2, 7) **h.** (11, 6)
  2. Melika
  3. a. Jalisa **b.** 3 blocks east and 4 blocks north
  4. a. 4 blocks **b.** 7 blocks **c.** 8 blocks **d.** 3 blocks
    e. 6 blocks **f.** 3 blocks **g.** 8 blocks **h.** 4 blocks
  5. Emily, Lauren, Raul, and Tia walk to school.
Describing Answers may vary.

Line Symmetry **66**

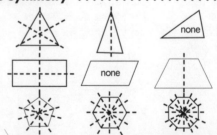

Expanding A regular polygon with n sides will have n lines
of symmetry.

    0-7424-1825-1 *Problem Solving*

Answer Key

Reflections **67**
   1–4. Check students' drawings.
   5. The size and shape of the image and its reflection is the same.
Comparing Answers may vary. Students should notice that these are similar concepts. When the reflecting line is placed so that it touches the edge of a shape, the reflection and its image can be considered one figure with a line of symmetry.

Rotations **68**

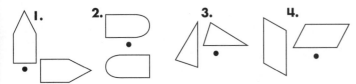

Comparing The size and shape of each image and its rotation is the same.

Translations **69**

1.

Image	Translation
A. (2, 7)	(6, 7)
B. (2, 9)	(6, 9)
C. (4, 9)	(8, 9)
D. (4, 7)	(8, 7)

2.

Image	Translation
A. (2, 7)	(4, 4)
B. (2, 9)	(4, 6)
C. (4, 9)	(6, 6)
D. (4, 7)	(6, 4)

3.

Image	Translation
E. (2, 1)	(5, 1)
F. (5, 1)	(8, 1)

4. A face was drawn by using the same shapes. The shapes were moved to different locations to create the picture.
Expanding Translating to the right makes the *x*-coordinate go up. Translating to the right and down changes both the *x*- and *y*-coordinates. If the point (x, y) is translated 4 units right, the *x*-coordinate will go up by 4. The translation point will be $(x + 4, y)$.

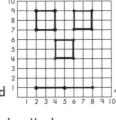

Toothpick Troubles **70**
   1. a. 4   **b.** 8   **2.**   **3.**

Expanding Answers will vary.

Mosaic Madness **71**
   1–2. Answers will vary.
Reflecting Answers may vary. Encourage students to realize that the designers somehow used mathematics to make sure the blocks fit.

Tiling Patterns **72**
   1. a. 360° **b.** The shapes have to fit around a point without gaps or overlaps. This means the shapes form a circle around the point. A circle is 360°.
   2. a. When arranged around the point, there is a gap between the shapes. **b.** The sum of the angles is 330°. Since this is less than 360°, the shapes will leave a gap. **c.** A tiling pattern will be possible only if the angles used around the point add up to exactly 360°.
Expanding The shape would have to have an angle measurement of 30° to make a tiling pattern (360 − 330 = 30). An isosceles triangle would fit, but the third side would be less than 1 inch. It might be difficult to expand this tiling pattern across a flat surface.

To Tile or Not to Tile **73–74**
   1. Yes. A square has 4 equal sides and 4 equal angles (90°).
   2. a. Yes. **b.** 4 **c.** 90° **d.** 360° **e.** Every angle of a square is 90°. To tile, multiple squares must fit around a point, with their angle measures totaling 360°. Since 360 ÷ 90 = 4, we know 4 angles of 90° will fit around a point. So 4 squares make a tiling pattern.
   3. a. Yes. All the sides are the same and all the angles are the same. **b.** 120° **c.** Yes. 3 triangles will create a tiling pattern. 360 ÷ 120 = 3. **d.** Check students tiling patterns.
   4. a. Answers may vary. **b.** No. 360 ÷ 108 = 3.3. The angle measure of a pentagon does not go into 360 evenly, which means there will be gaps or overlaps using only pentagons.
Explaining If the angle measure of a regular polygon goes into 360 evenly, a tiling pattern can be created using only that shape. If it does not, there will be gaps or overlaps.

Timely Tiling **75**
   1. a. 60° **b.** Yes. You can use 1 hexagon and 4 triangles (120 + 4 x 60 = 360) or 2 hexagons and 2 triangles (2 x 120 + 2 x 60 = 360). **c.** Answers will vary. **d.** Answers will vary.
   2. No combination of 108° and 120° angles will fit into 360° evenly. A hexagon and pentagon together will create a 228° angle (108 + 120), leaving a gap of 132° (360 − 228). One more hexagon or pentagon could be placed around the point, but there will still be a gap (360 − 228 − 120 = 12 or 360 − 228 − 108 = 24).
Expanding Answers will vary.

Check Your Skills **77**
   1. a. right isosceles **b.** obtuse scalene **c.** equilateral (acute)
   2. All angles in an equilateral triangle measure 60°. All equilateral triangles are acute.
   3. 900° (7 − 2 = 5; 5 x 180 = 900)
   4. Prisms have 2 bases while pyramids only have 1 base. Prisms have rectangular faces, but pyramids have triangular faces. Pyramids have a vertex, and prisms don't.

   0-7424-1825-1 *Problem Solving*

Answer Key

5. a. Yes. 2 squares and 3 equilateral triangles form a tiling pattern since their angle measures add up to 360° (90 + 90 + 60 + 60 + 60 = 360). **b.** No. An octagon's angle will not go into 360 evenly (360 ÷ 135 = 2.7).
c. Yes. Use 1 hexagon, 1 square, and the 150° angle of the parallelogram (120 + 90 + 150 = 360).

Estimating Will Do 78–79
1. Answers will vary.
2. a. 6.6 cm by 15.5 cm **b.** 102.3 cm² **c.** area
d. Answers will vary. **e.** Answers will vary. ($A = l \times w$)
f. area **g.** Answers will vary. Divide the area of the desk by 102.3.
3. Answers will vary.
4. The calculation and test should be about the same.
5. a–c. Answers will vary.
6. area of floor ÷ 102.3 = number of dollar bills that will cover the floor

Reflecting It would take a long time to cover the floor with dollar bills. This would also be expensive if you were using real dollar bills! Students should be confident in their calculation method. Testing isn't necessary.

Fencing In 80
1. a. 340 ft. **b.** The 5 ft. fencing panels will work best. Five is a factor of both 50 and 120. None of the 5 ft. panels will have to be cut. **c.** 68 fence panels will be needed, (50 ÷ 5 = 10; 10 x 2 = 20; 120 ÷ 5 = 24; 24 x 2 = 48; 48 + 20 = 68).
2. 12 m   **3.** 1,200 ft.
Reflecting perimeter

Rectangular Reasoning 81–82
1. Multiple answers are possible.
2. The sum of the length and width must be half the perimeter.
3. Multiple answers are possible.
4. $l + w = 16$ **5.** $l + w = 20$
6. $l + w = \frac{1}{2}P$ **7.** Answers will vary. $A = l \times w$
8. Answers will vary.
9.

length (ft.)	1	2	3	4	5	6	7	8	9	10	11	12	13	14	15
width (ft.)	15	14	13	12	11	10	9	8	7	6	5	4	3	2	1
area (ft.²)	15	28	39	48	55	60	63	64	63	60	55	48	39	28	15

10. a. length = 8 ft. **b.** width = 8 ft.
Reflecting A square will always give the largest area for any perimeter.

Confounding Confetti 83
1. a. 128 square centimeters
b. $A = \frac{1}{2} l \times w = \frac{1}{2} \times 16 \times 16 = 128$ square centimeters
c. area
2. a. 18 **b.** 18 x 128 = 2,304 cm³ **c.** volume
Explaining Find the area of the base ($A = \frac{1}{2} \times b \times h$). Then, multiply the area of the base by the height of the container.

Calling All Units 84
1. 1 inch is approximately 2.5 cm.
2.

Object	Measurement	Units
binder width	8.5	in.
binder length	28	cm
desk top width	60	cm
desk top length	18	in.
desk height	36	in.
door width	30	in.
door height	210	cm

3. binder length = 28 cm ÷ 2.5 = 11.2 in.
desk top width = 60 cm ÷ 2.5 = 24 in.
door height = 210 cm ÷ 2.5 = 84 in.
Describing Answers may vary.

A Matter of Time 85
1. 168 hours (24 hours/day x 7 days)
2. Answers may vary. 7 hours a day x 5 days = 35 hours per week.
3. Answers may vary. 8 hours a night x 7 nights = 56 hours per week. 56 hours per week x 52 weeks per year = 2,912 hours a year.
4. Answers may vary. 168 hours in a week; 35 + 56 = 91 hours in school and sleeping; 168 − 91 = 77 hours doing other things
5. Answers may vary. In school = $\frac{35}{168}$ = 20.8%.
Sleeping = $\frac{56}{168}$ = 33.3%. Other = $\frac{77}{168}$ = 45.8%
Reflecting To answer these questions, you need to know the number of hours in a day, the number of days in a week, and the number of weeks in a year.

The Temperature Is Rising 86
Reverse Formula: subtract 30 and then divide by 1.8.
1. 10° C   **2.** 75° F
3. 93° F; swimming   **4.** 28°– 36° C
Reflecting Answers will vary.

Weighty Matters 87
1. 27.3 kg (60 ÷ 2.2)
2. 24.2 lb. (11 x 2.2)
3. 2,727.3 kg (3 x 2,000 = 6,000 lb.; 6,000 ÷ 2.2 = 2,727.3)
4. 8.8 T. (8,000 x 2.2 = 17,600 lb.; 17,600 ÷ 2,000 = 8.8)
Explaining Divide by 2.2 to convert from pounds to kilograms. Multiply by 2.2 to convert from kilograms to pounds.

Lively Liquids 88
1. 7.6 liters (2 gal x 3.8 L/gal.)
2. 52.6 gallons (200 L ÷ 3.8 L/gal.)
3. 786.6 liters (1,656 pt. ÷ 8 pt./gal = 207 gal; 207 gal. x 3.8 liters/gal. = 786.6 L)
Reflecting Problem 3 required more than 1 step. This occurs when you do not have the conversion factor for the given units (pints to liters). You must first convert pints to gallons and then convert gallons to liters.

118

Answer Key

The Better Buy 89

1. The bag of apples is a better deal. Each apple costs
$3.00 ÷ 24 = $0.125, which is less than the single price
of $0.15 per apple.

2. The 24 oz. size is the better buy ($0.128 per oz. vs.
$0.139 per oz.).

3. a. 7 panels will be needed (18 x 30 = 540 in.²;
3,456 ÷ 540 = 6.4). **b.** 4 panels will be needed
(36 x 24 = 864 in.²; 3,456 ÷ 864). **c.** The smaller panels
are the better buy. Small panels cost $0.08 per square inch
($42.89 ÷ 540). Large panels cost $0.10 per square inch
($86.90 ÷ 864). **d.** 7 small panels will cost $300.23
($42.89 x 7).

Explaining Divide the price of each item by its size to find the
price per unit. Then compare unit prices.

Check Your Skills 91

1. 36 index cards (24 in. x 36 in. = 864 in.²;
4 in. x 6 in. = 24 in.²; 864 ÷ 24 = 36)

2. a. 16 ft. by 16 ft. **b.** 256 ft.²

3. 8.3° C   **4.** 4,545.5 kg

5. 50 gallons **6.** 8 pt. ($0.53 per qt. vs. $0.60 per qt.)

At the Movies 92

1.

2. 4th grade: comedy and action; 5th grade: horror

3. The same number of fourth- and fifth-grade students liked
action movies. Most fifth-grade students prefer horror movies.
Horror movies are the least favorite among fourth-grade
students.

Comparing More fourth-grade students liked comedy and
drama than fifth-grade students. An equal number of fourth- and
fifth-grade students liked action movies. Many more fifth-grade
students than fourth-grade students chose horror movies.

Favorite Sport 93

Answers will vary depending on survey results.

Organizing Answers will vary depending on students'
background knowledge. They could have made a double line
graph or back-to-back stem-and-leaf plots.

How Do You Get to School? 94

1. a. walk = 90°; car = 72°; bus = 162°; bike = 36°

b.

2. Answers will vary.

Explaining Change the percentage to a decimal by moving the
decimal two places to the left. Then multiply the decimal by
the number.

Favorite Season 95

Answers will vary depending on survey results.

Reflecting All categories should add up to 100%, which means
every section of the circle graph should be labeled.

Everyone's a Critic 96

1. *The Rise of the Zombies* received the worst ratings. Only 2
critics rated the movie with a 3. All the other ratings were
below a 3. It also has the lowest mean (1.4), median (1), and
mode (1 and 2) score.

2. *A Day to Remember* would have the best chance for an
Academy Award nomination. Most all of the critics rated it
highly. It also has the highest mean (3.8), median (4), and
mode (5) score.

3. The critics were split on *Slapstick Joe*. It had 6 very low and
6 very high rankings, with only 3 middle rankings.

4. There were a total of 15 critics.

Describing Answers will vary. Encourage students to mention
peaks, symmetry, and skew.

In the News 97

1. Headline 1 uses the mean. Headline 2 uses the median.
Headline 3 uses the mode.

2. The added property would change the mean to $105,000
and the median to $100,000. The mode would not change,
since $40,000 still occurs the most.

Expanding Answers will vary.

Test Scores 98

1. 45, 55, 59, 62, 67, 68, 70, 72, 75, 76, 77, 80, 81, 85, 88,
89, 91, 95, 100

2. 76   **3.** 67   **4.** 88   **5.** no

Expanding 25% is below the first quartile; 50% is below the
median; 75% is below the third quartile; 50% is between the first
and third quartile

Standing in Line 99-100

1. Answers may vary.

2. a. 3 **b.** 2 **c.** 1 **d.** 3 x 2 x 1 = 6

3. a. DJT; DTJ; JDT; JTD; TJD; TDJ **b.** 6 **c.** yes

4. a. LKAM; LKMA; LAMK; LAKM; LMAK; LMKA;
KALM; KAML; KMAL; KMLA; KLAM; KLMA;

0-7424-1825-1 *Problem Solving*

Answer Key

ALKM; ALMK; AKLM; AKML; AMKL; AMLK
MAKL; MALK; MKAL; MKLA; MLAK; MLKA

b. $4 \times 3 \times 2 \times 1 = 24$

Comparing Answers will vary. The formula helps find the number of different possibilities. The cubes help you list the possibilities.

Keep on Rolling 101

1. Answers will vary.

2. Answers may vary somewhat. They should come out about equal.

3.

Diana's Die

Kida's Die +	1	2	3	4	5	6
1	2	3	4	5	6	7
2	3	4	5	6	7	8
3	4	5	6	7	8	9
4	5	6	7	8	9	10
5	6	7	8	9	10	11
6	7	8	9	10	11	12

4. You are most likely to roll a 7. You are least likely to roll a 2 or 12.

5. Both have an equal chance of winning.

Expanding $\frac{6}{36} = \frac{1}{6}$. The chart shows 36 possible roll combinations. Of these, 6 of them are doubles.

Random Draw 102

Bag 1: 3 blue, 3 yellow, 3 green, 1 red
Bag 2: 5 blue, 3 red, 1 green, 1 yellow
Bag 3: 4 blue, 3 red, 2 green, 1 yellow
Reflecting Answers will vary.

Spin Out 103

1. Answers will vary.

2. Answers may vary. The person with the even sum has a slightly better chance of winning. ($\frac{13}{25}$ vs. $\frac{12}{25}$)

3. The person with the even sum. (It is possible the even sum will not win. The more spins you use in a game, the better the chance the person with the even sum will win.)

4.

	1	2	3	4	5
1	2	3	4	5	6
2	3	4	5	6	7
3	4	5	6	7	8
4	5	6	7	8	9
5	6	7	8	9	10

5. There are 13 even sums and 12 odd sums.

Extending There are 16 even sums and 9 odd sums. The player with the even sum has a much better chance of winning now.

	1	2	3	4	5
1	2	2	3	4	5
2	3	4	6	8	10
3	4	6	9	12	15
4	5	8	12	16	20
5	6	10	15	20	25

Check Your Skills 105

1. a. A pie chart would be best to display this data. The pie chart will show percentages of the whole. **b.** Answers will vary. Make sure students' angle measurements correspond to their percentages.

2. a. mean = 75.9, median = 75, mode = 77
b. lower quartile = 63; upper quartile = 89

3. 120 ways ($5 \times 4 \times 3 \times 2 \times 1$)

4. 6 red, 2 blue, 1 green, 1 yellow

Cumulative Post Test 106–107

1. 31, 73, and 83; 39, 42, and 69 are divisible by 3. 77 is divisible by 11. 31, 73, and 83 are not divisible by any of the digits 2–9. They also are not divisible by other prime numbers.

2. Answers may vary.

3. Band = 24, Gym = 30, Classrooms = 36, Art = 30

4. 22 students

5. 4, 12, 36, 108, 324, 972; Rule: × 3

6. Mara first, Alys second, Lourdes third, and Chu fourth

7. trapezoid = 9, triangle = 5, hexagon = 10

8. $P = 25T + 2$

9. 1,260° ($9 - 2 = 7$; $7 \times 180 = 1,260$)

10. No. 140 does not go into 360 evenly.

11. 9' × 9'; a square gives the maximum area

12. 51.6° F

13. 36 oz. ($0.095 per oz. vs. $0.107 per oz.)

14. double bar graph

15. 24 ($4 \times 3 \times 2 \times 1 = 24$)

 0-7424-1825-1 *Problem Solving*

sum

difference

growing patterns

decreasing patterns

area

perimeter

0-7424-1825-1 *Problem Solving*

answer to a subtraction problem

$$124$$
$$- 113$$
$$\boxed{11}$$

answer to an addition problem

$$214$$
$$+ 312$$
$$\boxed{526}$$

a series of numbers that gets smaller using a rule

35 33 32 30
Rule: –2

a series of numbers that gets larger using a rule

4 8 12 16 20
Rule: +4

distance around a shape

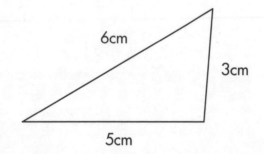

6cm

3cm

5cm

3 + 5 + 6 = 14 cm

amount of space inside a shape

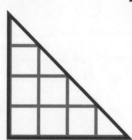

8 square units

0-7424-1825-1 *Problem Solving*

line
symmetry

reflection

rotation

translation

volume

tiling
pattern

0-7424-1825-1 *Problem Solving*

flipping a shape across a line

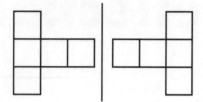

ability to divide a shape into two identical, mirror-image halves

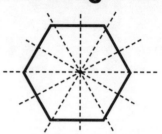

sliding a shape to a new location

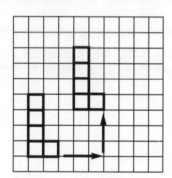

turning a shape

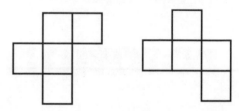

90° clockwise rotation

when shapes fit together around a single point without any gaps or overlaps

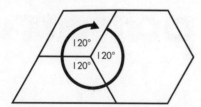

amount of space inside a 3-dimensional object

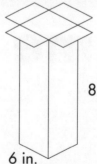

8 in.   **6 x 6 x 8 =**

288 in.³

6 in.

prisms

pyramids

polygon

quadrilateral

parallelogram

regular
polygon

0-7424-1825-1 *Problem Solving*

3-dimensional shape
- **I polygon base**
- **triangular faces**
- **point**

3-dimensional shape
- **2 identical polygon bases**
- **rectangular faces**

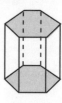

polygon with 4 sides

closed shape with straight edges

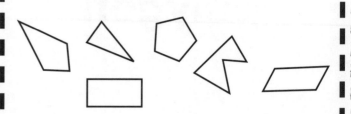

all sides are congruent and all angles are congruent

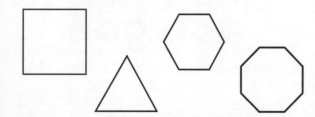

quadrilateral where opposite sides are congruent and parallel

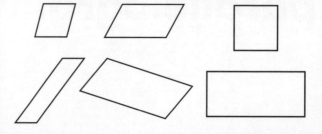

0-7424-1825-1 *Problem Solving*

mean	median
mode	quartiles
double bar graph	pie chart

0-7424-1825-1 *Problem Solving*

the middle number in a group of ordered data

2, 3, 4, 5, ⑥ 7, 7, 7, 8

the average number in a group of data

2, 3, 4, 5, 6, 7, 7, 7, 8

2 + 3 + 4 + 5 + 6 + 7 + 7 + 7 + 8 = 49

49 ÷ 9 = ⑤.④

the middle numbers of the lower and upper halves in a group of ordered data

1, 2, ③, 4, 5, ⬚6⬚, 7, 7, ⑦, 8, 9

1st = 3; 3rd = 7

the number occurring most often in a group of data

2, 3, 4, 5, 6, ⑦, 7, 7, 8

circular graph used to show category percentages

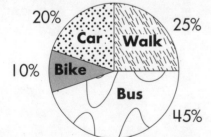

graph used to compare 2 different groups in multiple categories

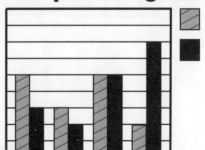

0-7424-1825-1 *Problem Solving*